skills for the youngest learners

SKI TIPS for KIDS

fun instructional techniques with cartoons!

Zoom!

written & illustrated by
Mike Clelland!
with Alex Evere

FALCON GUIDES

GUILFORD, CONNECTICUT
HELENA, MONTANA

AN IMPRINT OF GLOBE PEQUOT PRESS

FALCONGUIDES®

FalconGuides is an imprint of Globe Pequot Press.

Falcon, FalconGuides, and Outfit Your Mind are registered trademarks of Morris Book Publishing, LLC.

Illustrations: Mike Clelland!

Project Editors: Tracee Williams and Lauren Brancato
Layout: Joanna Beyer

Library of Congress Cataloging-in-Publication Data is available on file.

ISBN 978-0-7627-8000-6

Printed in the United States of America

10 9 8 7 6 5 4 3 2 1

Contents

Acknowledgments

I don't have any kids myself, nor have I ever taught any kids to ski, but I sure know how to draw them. I see teaching children as something visual, and in to the following pages you'll see and read a foundation for skiing that should be fun. This book would never have made it into your hands if it weren't for Alex Everett. I am indebted to his insights and thoughtful ways. We would also like to thank the following folks for their passion for skiing with children and their assistance with this project. We are filled with gratitude for all the help we so generously received.

Nato Emerson, Caryl Everett, Ryan Haight, Beth Imes, Ted Imes, Tuffy Kaiser, Rich McLaughlin, Danielle Petriccione, Melissa Pangraze, Anne Schorling, James Thompson, John Burbidge, George Moser, Corey McGrath, The Bergstrom's (Mark, Liz, Orion and Phoebe), Molly and Avery Absolon, Allen O'Bannon, Stephen and Jonah Lisa Dyer, Kristen Lummis, The Ski School at Grand Targhee, Tony and Deb Jewell, Scott and Bechler Bossel, Rich Renadi, Tracey Everett, and Erika Earles.

Introduction

Ski Tips for Kids is meant to be simple and fun to use. It's got oodles of cartoons for kids and lots of words for adults who are teaching their little ones to ski. Though it's designed for parents who have good skiing skills and want to help young first-time skiers, it's also a great resource for adults with less experience on the slopes who want to share in the learning process along with their children.

The text is short and sweet, without too many big words, so any grown-up should be able to read it out loud to kids. The illustrations are fun, but, at the same time, they are detailed and instructional. The goal is to give both kids and adults a visual learning guide as a way to gain beginner skills and eventually progress to more challenging slopes. Even though this book is full of silly cartoons, the actual skills are a rock solid foundation for *anyone* new to skiing.

We encourage you to spend some time with your kids reading this book well before the start of ski season. You can even carry this book with you on the slopes. Hopefully it will help you and your child build a strong knowledge base for a lifetime of skiing!

Skiing is fun

There is nothing more magical than gliding on snow with skis on your feet! It's the kind of fun that electrifies the soul. This book has plenty of tips and insights on how to teach this life-long skill. But you should always put fun first! Be ready to put this book away for a while if the teaching and learning isn't fun and you and your child grow frustrated. It's important to make sure that *fun* is the absolute centerpiece of the whole shebang! Sometimes that means abandoning the ski hill for the day and heading to the hotel swimming pool, or back home to do something else. Stopping before anybody gets miserable is an important part of keeping everybody psyched for the next time out.

When to start?

There is no "perfect age" for starting kids on skis. From about 1½ to 2 years old is about the earliest a child can attempt to ski. At this age, simply focus on fun in the snow and keep teaching to a bare minimum. Expect (maybe) 30 minutes of playing and sliding around. At this age, simple plastic strap-on skis may be fine.

The threshold for most organized ski schools' lessons is potty training, which tends to be between 2½ and 3 years old. Children at this age are able to ski for extended periods and can progress quickly with patient instruction.

Just because some kids start as young as 2½ years old doesn't mean they have to. So please don't think that this book is advocating that you start 'em that early. At that age there isn't really too much they can do. They'll tire out easily and there might be some tears. Nothing will be lost if you wait till they are 4 or 5 years old. At that point they'll be at an age where they are a little stronger and can progress a little faster.

The benefits of ski school lessons

Lessons can be an important supplement to your own efforts. In the first few minutes of a lesson, an experienced youth ski instructor will begin to assess a child's mindset and physical abilities. They'll use these observations along with input from the child and parents to tailor a ski lesson that will be fun, safe, and successful. Instructors are professionals who do this all winter long. They have the big-picture knowledge for leading little students through the right challenges at the right time.

Youth ski instructors will keep a watchful eye on the mood and energy level of their students, and when they sense that it's time to take a break from skiing, they'll shift to other activities like looking for animal tracks, building a snowman, or heading inside for a quick warm-up and some hot chocolate. An instructor can be particularly helpful with a child who has never-ever been on skis, making those first few hours fun and productive when everything is new and potentially overwhelming.

Most ski areas offer a range of lessons including group lessons, private lessons, and specialized ski camps. A group lesson will include three to eight students of a similar age and skill level. These lessons are the most affordable, and being in a group means making new friends; a crew of kids all skiing together can be super fun and motivating. A downside of the group setting is that each student will receive less individual attention and—due to safety concerns—the lesson will be geared to the lowest skill level in the group.

Private lessons have the benefit of intensive one-on-one coaching and guiding that is geared to the individual. The lesson will be tailored to the needs of the student. If you are interested, most ski instructors are happy to work with parents and kids together in a private lesson setting. An experienced youth ski instructor can help guide the family through the rental process and will make sure that the child has all of the correct gear, snacks, and sunscreen for the lesson. You'll get to observe how the instructor teaches your child and you'll pick up some tips and vocabulary you can use later. If you're planning to teach your own child to ski, this can be a great way to jumpstart the process for both of you. This requires good communication between the parents and instructor, and parents should be prepared to respect the instructor's judgment on how to best tailor the lesson. Be aware that sometimes the presence of the parents can be a distraction. The instructor will need some time to develop a rapport with the child before the parents enter the scene.

While instructors in both group and private lessons will provide a lesson summary and tips for next steps, the private lesson instructor can be expected to have more details and insights to share with parents after the lesson.

Many ski areas offer ski camps, particularly over busy holiday periods. Camps usually involve a multi-day series of lessons and activities specially focused on teaching a big-picture progression of skills. Ski camps at some resorts might offer organized kid-centric activities in the evening like games and movies.

Preparing for a successful lesson

Before you arrive for a lesson, make sure your child is well rested, well fed, and ready for a fun day outside. The instructor will want to talk with the parents and find out as much as possible about their child's skiing ability and interests. Are they a never-ever? Have they been on the chairlift? Maybe they tried skiing once before and they were cold and scared. Or, maybe they are really excited to ski, but they're a little shy. All instructors have had some challenging days when this baseline info wasn't shared and the lesson wasn't as fun or successful as it could have been. Thoughtful input from the child's parents helps enormously.

Set goals for the day and share them with the instructor. For example: Our daughter would love to be able to ski with her friends and the friends' parents, but needs to work on confidence and skiing a little faster. Or, our son loves zooming straight down the hill and doesn't think turning is necessary.

Be prepared to pass on information about allergies, special food needs, or any medical issues. This is basic safety information that any instructor will want to know before beginning a lesson.

At the end of the lesson, the instructor will be eager to talk to the parents to give an account of the day. Where'd we go? What did we work on? What tips worked for your child? Did they have fun, listen, get along? Are they excited about doing it again? Instructors really want to share what worked well in the lesson and good instructors view parents as partners in teaching their children to ski. Instructors will be able to reinforce the content of the lesson and outline the next steps for building more skills and keeping the ball rolling, things like what terrain to try or avoid, what techniques to encourage, and what games to play. Most ski areas will have a report card or skills guide that kids can take home to keep track of their progress.

And remember, it's a courtesy to tip the instructors! They work hard for low pay.

DEFINE LEARNING STYLES:

The voice in this book is mostly directed at the adult who is playing the role of teacher; you'll get insights into the mentoring process.

But in other places, especially in the last third of the book, that voice changes so that it talks directly to the little skier. Pretty much anytime there is a tip meant to describe a specific skill, it'll be voiced for the learner. Remember, these ski instructions can be read aloud.

make sure to use
ALL THREE STYLES!

TIPS FOR TEACHERS

The role of the teacher

Whether you teach your child from day one or ski with them after lessons, you will have a huge influence on how they think, feel, and progress with skiing. The more tools and tips you have, the better.

Here's an important question: What's your own skill level? Are you a good enough skier to teach safely and effectively? If you aren't a strong skier yourself, you'll be in way over your head if you try to teach these subtle skills to a child. *You need to be a very good skier yourself if you want to play the role of instructor.* Most important, if you don't have strong skiing skills, do *not* take your kid on the chairlift!

Part of your role as an instructor will be to role-model the skills you'll be teaching. This means you can clearly demonstrate what you are asking the kids to do. You'll need to be comfortable enough to have fun and skilled enough to sidestep or skate uphill *without* poles. You'll be picking up a fallen little skier on a slippery slope and helping them through the lift line and onto the chairlift all without getting tangled up. This is a tall order if you don't have a good baseline of strong skiing skills yourself.

There are plenty of tips in the following pages for those parents who are on this path.

Enjoy the moment

If there is any kind of mantra for this book, it's this: *Skiing is fun!* Never let this core concept stray from your mind.

Skiing is a lifetime sport, so there's no need to rush anything. Remember, skiing simply means sliding around on snow. But in the beginning it can feel complicated and overwhelming. The role of the ski instructor is just to show the student that playing in the snow is fun. Skiing is just one part of that fun, but it shouldn't be the sole focus.

The Buddhists teach of non-attachment, and when you're skiing with a child it might be a good idea to wear your Zen hat. Enter into the experience without fixed expectations.

It is common to spend a week prepping for a ski day, drive for hours to the resort, and then rent gear. When you finally get all the winter clothes and skis on, the child might do one run and say that's enough. This might happen and you need to be prepared to just roll with it.

Tips for Teachers

Everything will take longer with kids, sometimes a *lot* longer. Even the simplest thing (like putting on the skis) can end up feeling super complicated. Be forewarned, this is normal. If you are rushing and impatient, they'll sense that. Having a light-hearted attitude is essential.

Be aware of frustration levels, both in the child *and* the teacher. At the first inkling of any change in the mood just back off, take a break, or get the chocolate out. This might mean going in, getting warm, and drinking hot cocoa. Or, it might mean no teaching at all, just fun ski time.

For the most part, kids don't get too discouraged by falling—that's more of an adult thing—but there are plenty of other things that can lead to a meltdown, like not being able to keep up with a big brother, or not getting to choose the next trail. Be aware that when the snow is deep, little kids will have a hard time plowing through it. This can be really frustrating. One of the great arts of the ski instructor is to be able to divert attention from these sources of frustration and keep the experience focused on fun and learning.

Here's a truism: *Frustration and skiing are a miserable pairing.*

Expect lots of breaks

Kids require eating, drinking, and resting. They may not tell you when they want to go in, so make sure to ask 'em how they are doing. Better yet, if you think it is time to take a break, take one. It may not be obvious when your little skier is tucked away behind goggles and helmet.

Check in often, that way you'll have a heads-up for their needs ahead of time. Lift lines, riding the chair, skiing down a long run, and getting back to the lodge all take longer than expected. If they want a break, you need to respect that.

Make sure your kids are fueled up throughout the day. Pre-load their pockets with a few granola bars or other snacks. Parents can keep a thermos of hot chocolate in a pocket or backpack. Take breaks just to drink water. And always pee before you ski!

PEE BEFORE YOU SKI!

NORMAL
SKIING IN
PROPER BODY POSE

WIGGLE DANCE!

Yelling WIGGLE DANCE
means everybody shakes
their GROOVE THING for
three seconds!
(acting silly is good)

Support, encourage, coach

Give plenty of encouragement and praise. If they fall in the snow make sure to say, "You did great! Don't worry about falling, everybody falls! That was so awesome!" Celebrate any little accomplishment. When in doubt, heap on more praise.

Be silly, sing songs, play games, and smile! Your children will be reading your expression—if you're nervous, they will be too. If you are having fun, so will they.

At the same time, be sure to give the child accurate feedback. Soothe them if they fall, but give them some simple, positive coaching on why they fell. Kids will have fun with these quick, easy-to-use tips.

Refine the skills with lots of time on easy terrain. Find ways to explore in places that present new challenges in small increments. If medium-sized turns on the groomed Green slope are becoming routine, try mixing up short little turns in and around some widely spaced trees.

All too often parents (especially ones who are hardcore skiers themselves) will take kids to the next level of steeper terrain before they are ready. Parents need to be very patient and avoid pushing the children beyond their ability. It might feel hard for parents to spend all day on the bunny slope, but it's worth it. If a child gets scared on new, harder terrain, learning and fun shut down. Ski instructors use this mantra: *Over-TRAIN before over-TERRAIN'ing.*

Use your children's imagination to improvise and play. Enter a fantasy world of inspiration. Sneak into the trees and imagine another world, full of adventure. Create an imaginative realm with your young skier. This can be your greatest gift as a teacher, getting them engaged in creative fun while they are skiing outside in a beautiful wintery place.

Short skis for the grown-ups!

The kids will be skiing on short little skis, and you should consider doing this too. Short skis make getting around on the bunny slopes a lot easier, because you'll probably be climbing back uphill over and over. Short skis make getting in close to the child simpler, especially when your edges are perpendicular to the fall line. Plus, as a mentor you'll probably be skiing without poles and this is easier on short skis.

BIG ADULT

NO POLES

tiny SKIS

No need to max out the credit card on a high-performance set of dinky boards. Any ski town will have a secondhand store with cheap old gear. Keep your eyes open for garage sales, or just rent a pair of short skis for the days you're playing teacher.

It's nice to use short little skis when teaching little kids!

Skiing backward as a teacher

Are you skilled enough to safely ski backward on the bunny slope? If so, you are set up well to teach kids. There are oodles of ways that skiing backward can help in your role as teacher.

But, be careful! The worst thing you could do while skiing backward is to run into another tiny learner. You'll need to constantly look over both shoulders to make sure you aren't going to collide with anyone. Skiing backward is pretty easy with short skis, and you won't really go that fast.

If you can't ski backward, just pop your skis off and walk backward (or just alongside). This works wonderfully for the newest and youngest beginners because you can usually walk as fast as they ski. Without skis it is easy to get in close and help your children to get back up. But, they still need someone to demonstrate what to do on skis, so if you have a partner, one person can ski and the other can walk. Be aware, there will quickly come a time when they can ski a lot faster than you can walk!

WALKING BACKWARD might be easier than skiing backward!

...or just walk along beside them!

(walking forward)

Parents skiing together

If you can get a group of parents together with a few kids, you can share the duties of watching the kids. The adults can rotate time teaching and playing with the little folks while the others can ski for themselves.

Work as a team and divide up the roles. One parent can stay in the lodge or on the bunny slope while the others ski a few runs. Make a plan to switch out as needed. Cell phones make this easier for everyone.

Kids are different from adults

An adult's *center of mass* is around the belly button. The center of mass for kids is much higher (especially age 5 and younger) because their heads are huge compared to the rest of their body. Add a helmet and you bring that balance point up even higher. This means that when watching kids and evaluating their skiing, they won't conform to the adult ideal.

Kids will have distinctly different challenges with balance from grown-ups. There is a graceful full-body pose that a skilled adult skier will display on the slopes. The upper body is leaning forward in a strong athletic stance. A child's head is too big to match this same sturdy position; instead they'll look like they are leaning back a little bit.

Unlike kids, adults have lots of fine motor control in their ankles, hands, knees, and toes. This means subtle abilities over lots of different moving parts in their taller shape.

A child's body (particularly 2- to 4-year-olds), with short little arms and legs, will tend to move as one unit. They'll ski down the hill as one frozen block. Some of the skiing movements described later in the book (like ankle flexing or turning with the lower body) will be out of reach until they get a bit older.

That said, kids have some cool advantages over adults. One is that their smaller anatomy is all set up with bones and joints that are pliable and springy. When they fall they bend and twist into outlandish shapes. But pick 'em up, watch their legs and skis unwind like a helicopter, set 'em down, and off they go.

Mindset

It's hard to have fun if anyone is feeling:

~ too cold

~ too hot

~ too tired

~ too frustrated

~ too hungry

~ too thirsty

~ too much pressure

~ too overwhelmed

If you or your child is dealing with any of these feelings, back off and solve it!

ADULTS
can bend
and rotate
different parts
independently

KIDS
have a kinda
blocky body
position

Even though kids are smaller, they have bigger imaginations, so they appreciate little things like tiny jumps and narrow trails through tight trees. When you're only 40 inches tall, 6 inches of new snow is an epic powder day!

An important insight for teaching: Kids have some significant differences in perception. Their sense of space, or their *bubble of awareness*, is much smaller than an adult's. They tend to focus on what's right there in front of them.

When teaching it's important to get right in close in order to get their full attention. Also, it's tough for kids to *mirror* a teacher that's facing them (a normal teaching technique for adults). It's much better to be alongside or just in front. Most kids are better at mimicking your motions than trying to listen to a verbal explanation. Their learning process is more physical than intellectual. Learning happens by doing!

Parents (and kids) also need to be aware that there can be big differences between kids from year to year and even within children of the same age. Everyone develops physically and emotionally at their own rate. Everyone has a different learning style. Some like to eagerly jump in and try something right away, while others hold back. Anyone teaching kids has to be flexible and aware of how stuff is being received. Come prepared with a virtual grab bag of ideas and tricks to meet their needs. Don't get too locked into a formalized progression. If something is obviously more fun than something else—*by all means do that!*

Tips for Teachers

ADULT BODY POSITION
vs.
KIDS BODY POSITION

THE GEAR

Skis

Skis come in all shapes and sizes. Alpine skis have a curved-up tip in the front, a waist in the middle, and a tail in the back. They are shaped a little bit like an hourglass. This is called *side cut* and this shape helps the ski turn. The base of the ski is smooth, and when it's nicely waxed it will slide fast and easy. The edges of the ski are made of metal that can be sharpened so that it bites and carves the snow and the skier can turn and stop.

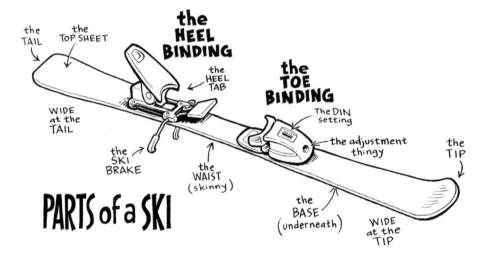

PARTS of a SKI

Plastic skis

You might see plastic skis that just strap on to a pair of winter boots. These are simple and inexpensive, but they aren't really the right tool for a ski area. Both the boots and the bindings are so loose that the child won't really have much control. The skis don't have a metal edge so they won't turn or stop well. These are really only an option for the *very* first day skiing and the *youngest* skiers.

The plastic strap-on skis might be better suited for the day you make a snowman in your own yard, or maybe a little sledding slope in the neighborhood. If you already have them, let your child play with them indoors! Put them on and let your son or daughter practice walking, stepping on the carpet.

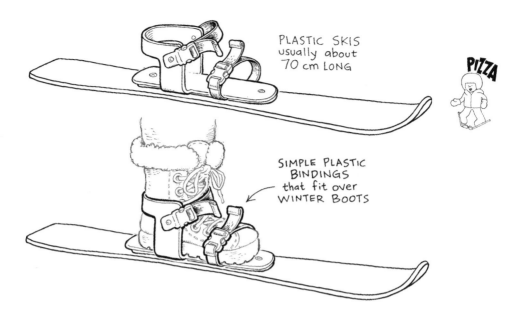

PLASTIC SKIS
usually about
70 cm LONG

PIZZA

SIMPLE PLASTIC
BINDINGS
that fit over
WINTER BOOTS

How to find skis for kids

There are lots of options for kids' ski gear, from buying it shiny and new to finding it at garage sales. Kids will grow out of their gear quickly, potentially before the next season, so keep your eyes open for any kinds of deals or look into sharing and trading with other families.

Rental gear for kids is usually very high quality. It's easy to get, either at the base area of the ski resort or at a ski shop in town. The staff at these places is skilled at fitting the boots, and rental prices for the smaller skis are a lot cheaper than adult gear.

Most resorts and ski shops offer deals on season-long rentals for junior skiers. If you think you'll be going more than once, this can be a great value, both in terms of money and the time you'll save by passing the rental lines. Also, if your kid graduates to longer skis or needs something a little different, they'll swap items out mid-season as part of the deal. Plus, they'll do most adjustments and repairs for free.

As their skills progress, kids will benefit from skis designed for specific skills and terrain. Most rental shops will have a range of skis for kids. This is a great way to demo some different designs and diversify the fun. Narrow, stiff skis are good for racing on groomed slopes; short twin-tip skis are perfect for the terrain park and doing tricks; and wider skis are good for exploring powder.

If you live in (or near) a ski town, there is usually a wealth of good kids' gear that gets handed around between families. This

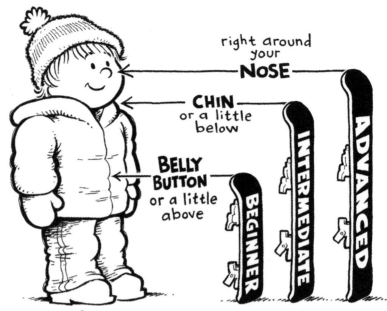

SIZING YER SKIS
a simple guideline

right around your **NOSE**

CHIN *or a little below*

BELLY BUTTON *or a little above*

BEGINNER

INTERMEDIATE

ADVANCED

gear shows up in secondhand stores, at garage sales, or can be obtained through word of mouth. Keep your eyes open during the off seasons. Kids are lighter and less aggressive than adults, so the wear and tear on the tiny gear is minimal. Skis and boots might have a few seasons on 'em, but they'll still look (and perform) like they're brand new.

Some ski areas (or ski shops) will provide a service where you can buy a full setup of gear and then trade it in each season, so as the child outgrows last year's equipment, they can just step into this year's gear. This is a really practical option.

Boots

Ski boots have a hard outer shell and a soft inner liner. The hard shells are nice and stiff so that any little move you make, like pressing your shins into the front of the boot, will become a message sent directly to the ski to help make it turn. The soft inner liner should be warm and comfortable, but snug.

There are two options for kids' boots. One is the traditional top entry, which can take some effort getting the little feet

Ski sizing

Height of skis to match a kid's skill level:

Absolute beginner–*first time on skis*–a little above their belly button

Intermediate–*got the basics of stopping and turning*–about at their chin

Advanced–*getting ready for the Blue runs*–about at their nose

INNER LINER fits inside

USUALLY only room for ONE BUCKLE

LOTSA TABS and FLAPS

HARD OUTER SHELL

SOFT INNER LINER

PIZZA

KIDS SKI BOOT SYSTEM

inside. The rear entry style tends to be a little easier to get on, especially for the youngest skiers.

For small children, comfort is more important than high performance. Boots are the most important piece of gear, and a proper fit is essential to the whole experience. Too tight and they'll get cold feet, too loose and they won't be able to control their skis. These aren't Olympic racers, so no need to squeeze 'em into tight form-fitting boots.

FOOT GOES HERE

REAR ENTRY BOOT

Putting on the boots

The youngest kids will need help, but the boot should slide on easily. Make sure there are no wrinkles or folds on the inside liner. Both socks need to be pulled up and wrinkle free. Long underwear should be pulled down smoothly over the socks. Every boot is different, but they all have funny plastic tabs and buckles that fold over each other in a specific order, and sometimes this can get complicated. The inner liner and the outer shell need to align perfectly without anything forced or pinched. If you're having trouble getting them on, pull the tongue way off to the side and spread the boot open wide. This should make it easier for a child to step into the boot.

Put the boots on inside the lodge where it's warm and you can adjust everything without gloves.

Boot fitting

All ski boots (kids and adults) are now using *Mondo* sizing. This is a universal sizing based on centimeters. The plastic outer shells are usually only in whole sizes, while the inner liners are in half sizes.

KIDS SKI BOOT SIZING CHART

USA kids size	MONDO size
8	14.5
9	15.5
10	16.5
11	17.5
12	18.5
13	19.5
1	20.5
2	21.5
3	22
4.5	22.5
5	23
5.5	23.5

Bindings

Bindings keep your boots attached to your skis. They have a front toe piece and a back heel piece. Both parts have a secret hidden spring that holds your boot in place while skiing, but it's smart enough to let go when you fall. Bindings even have brakes. These fold up out of the way when you're skiing, but pop down when you fall so that your skis don't zoom downhill without you.

You'll learn how to put them on and take them off in the next chapter.

The DIN scale

Ski bindings are adjusted to the size of the boot *and* the ability level of the skier. Bindings have an adjustable setting known as the DIN setting which will range from 0 to 5 for children. DIN is short for Deutsches Institut für Normung that translates to the German Institute for Standardization.

For beginners on gentle terrain at slower speeds, a low number means a loose setting that means it'll release easier with those awkward beginner falls. Bindings need to be adjusted more securely as you improve. Adding speed, variable snow conditions, and small bumps can cause the dreaded pre-release, so the DIN gets tightened and the numbers go up. Let the ski shop adjust the DIN, rather than trying to do it yourself.

Having the boot pop off from the binding while skiing can be frustrating and even dangerous. Keep an eye on how easily the bindings release, and don't hesitate to run them into the shop for a quick adjustment.

What about poles?

It's skis that make you a skier, not poles! First-time little skiers won't need poles. It's better to learn proper balance without 'em. They're tough for tiny hands to hold, and with so many other things to focus on, they just turn into a distraction. Also, they are totally unwieldy when trying to get on a chairlift with children.

If you are teaching kids (especially 2½ to 5-year-olds), *you should be doing it without poles too.* Being pole-free is essential when getting on and off the lift. You'll want your hands free to help those kids get loaded safely. Plus, you can get in close to help the little ones back up after a fall. Wait to add poles until they graduate to the more challenging Blue terrain.

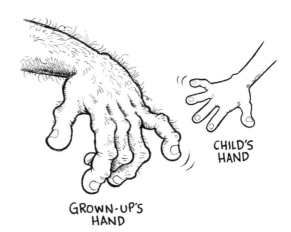

REMEMBER

CLIP!

ALWAYS
make sure
that your
HELMET
is
CLIPPED
ON!

Helmets

There is no rule or requirement about helmets, but they have become the absolute norm with kids. Helmets are cool!

Children might fall down and hit their head, but it's more likely that someone else might be skiing out of control and collide into them. Helmets will also keep a child's head warm and they're a good place for rad stickers.

Parents should role model safety (as well as being cool) by wearing a helmet too. Alas, most of the cartoons in this book show adults without helmets—that was the illustrator's fault.

Harnesses

Kid wrangling with some sort of harness and tether can solve a few problems. If you rig your children into some sort of harness system and then clip a cord to them, you can ski behind and control their speed. Some store-bought harnesses have two cords that clip to each side of their hips, and this can create a way for you to "steer" them while they are out in front of you.

Most professional ski instructors cringe at these tools because the child isn't learning good techniques, and it can be tough to break kids of the harness habit when the time comes. But, some parents love 'em because they can easily control the speed of the child. There isn't really a true *need* for this harness system, but it's an okay option for safety on larger slopes with more hazards.

Kids are pretty gung-ho, and they usually do just fine without any kind of harness. This can be more of a confidence-building tool for the parents, who like knowing that there is something there to keep their child from zooming out of control. Some parents realize that their kids may not listen to instructions, and these folks really like being able to rein in their fearless little speedsters.

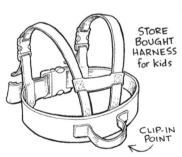

STORE
BOUGHT
HARNESS
for kids

CLIP-IN
POINT

Be aware that holding the tether tight will be teaching the children how to pull and not how to ski. Do your best to keep that cord just loose enough that they are truly skiing, but not so loose that reining 'em in means jerking 'em off balance. If they are pulling on the cord, they'll be leaning back too far instead of feeling the tongue of the boot.

Be careful on a crowded slope of beginners, 'cause that cord might snag someone else. Un-clip the tether from the harness and put it in a pocket before the chairlift ride.

DRESSING FOR WINTER

LONG UNDIES NEXT to SKIN

HAT

THICK insulating LAYER

SKI PANTS

NECK GAITER

PUFFY VEST

SKI SOCKS

I'm warm

HELMET

GOGGLES

MITTENS

SKI BOOTS

LAYERING for WINTER

(Some options for skiing)

Gloves and mittens

Mittens seem to work better than gloves for younger children. They are comfortable, easier to get on, and lots warmer. Look for mittens that have a long cuff that cinches or "Velcros" closed so that snow doesn't sneak in on the wrist. On really cold days, heat packs can be slipped into the mittens. Warm, sunny spring skiing might be the only time when gloves will work better than mittens.

Goggles

Wind, snow, and cold make it hard to see. Most kids do better with goggles than sunglasses. All ski helmets have some sort of clip on the back side to hold the goggle strap securely in place. It's easier for kids to put the goggles on the helmet first, and then put the helmet on their head. If the goggles are secure, they should stay on the helmet all day. Most important, *don't sit on them!*

Balaclava

Cover up those cheeks and noses on cold days with neck gaiters or balaclavas. Look for hats and balaclavas that are thin enough to fit easily underneath a helmet. The best are thin on top and fleecy around the face.

It is possible to pull the balaclava up onto the nose and around the eyes, then put the goggles on in a way that leaves no skin exposed. This is a good idea on the coldest days when any exposed skin can get numb and nipped by frost quickly. Make sure to check children's faces when it's cold and windy.

nice **BALACLAVA** for use with a **HELMET**

THICK FABRIC on the BOTTOM

THIN FABRIC on the TOP

Frostbite will show up as waxy white patches, usually on the tip of their noses or cheeks. Deal with this right away. Go inside and get warm. If you see this on the chairlift, you can cover their affected spot with your bare hand.

Another option for warmth is the combo of a hat and neck gaiter.

Socks

No need for thick (or multiple) socks–kids do better with one pair of thin socks. They should be snug enough to avoid wrinkles and tall enough to reach well above the height of the boot. You might need to reach in there a few times during the ski day and pull the socks up again. This smoothes out the wrinkles and improves comfort. Stay away from cotton socks! Kids'll be warmer and drier with wool or synthetic socks.

Tips for warm feet

~ Make sure the boots are dry! If you are on vacation and you are skiing day after day, it's *crucial* that the boots get dried out after each day of skiing.

~ Kids need wiggle room for their toes! The youngest skiers will lean back more than adults, and this will force the toes to the front. Pull the liners out, and have the kids put them on (with one thin sock) and then ask them to wiggle their toes. You'll be able to feel their toes and get a good idea how far they are from the front of the boot. A half inch of extra space is the minimum.

~ Make sure the boots and the feet are nice and warm *before* putting them on. Ski boots are like a thermos: They'll keep cold things cold and warm things warm.

~ Tucking the boots near a heater vent while driving to the ski area makes for toasty feet when the boots go on.

~ Pull the soft inner liners out of the shells each night and set them in a place where they are sure to dry out, like near a heater. The boots will dry quicker if you take the thin foot beds out for drying.

~ If you are skiing a lot, you might want to invest in an electric boot dryer!

KEEPING WARM

GOGGLES clip into the back of the HELMET

Some helmets have an **ADJUSTABLE BAND** on the inside for sizing

FUZZY FLEECE BALACLAVA for under the HELMET

I'M WARM!

ONLY the NOSE SHOWS

ALL the layers TUCKED IN nice & snug

BIG PARKA FITS OVER EVERYTHING!

fuzzy

FITS OVER HEAD

Warm

NECK GAITER

SKI BOOT DRYER

Remove the inner liner from the hard outer shell for quicker drying.

SOFT INNER LINER

Managing temperature

Skiing is a winter sport, and that means cold. But don't treat every ski day like it's the coldest day of the year. It's pretty common to see kids overdressed for the weather, and that means they'll overheat. It's hard to have fun when you're freezing cold or sweltering hot. Spring skiing can be freezing cold in the morning and broiling hot by the afternoon.

If your child is overheating, unzip and vent a jacket, remove and pocket a balaclava or neck gaiter. Or, run into the lodge and stash a layer. Keeping your child comfortable is always worth the extra effort because it keeps the focus on learning to ski!

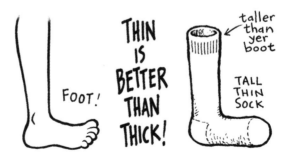

FOOT!

THIN IS BETTER THAN THICK!

taller than yer boot

TALL THIN SOCK

GETTING TO THE HILL

Before you even leave home

Skiing with little kids involves gobs of stuff and a lot of little details. All that gear needs to get into the car and forgetting even one little item might be a total bummer.

Make a checklist days before you plan on making a trip to the ski area. Include the kids in the creation of this list. Be super thorough. Skis and boots are easy to remember, but what about eating a good breakfast? Or dry socks for the drive home? An extra set of mittens in case the first set gets wet? Snacks for everyone? Enough tote bags to carry all the gear? A little favorite toy?

A good ski day with kids requires a nice slow pace and lowered expectations. You can't know how the day will proceed, and everything takes longer with kids. Plan to arrive early if you have a lesson. If you know the starting time is at 10 a.m., get to the ski area at 9. Don't bundle kids all the way up at home, because they'll get hot on the way. Do the bundling in the lodge immediately before going out to ski.

Before the skis go on

If you are teaching, you'll need to be at peace with a slow progression and repeating things over and over. Patience is essential. The good part is that most of the time kids will be having a ton of fun and that mood can be infectious!

Don't get too focused on the actual skiing. Be aware that each step along the way has its own challenges. Proceed forward calmly.

- ~ Step ONE: Get from the car to the lodge.

- ~ Step TWO: Find a bench and cubby space.

- ~ Step THREE: Get the tickets and get them attached.

- ~ Step FOUR: Get the boots on and get everyone ready for the day.

- ~ Step FIVE: Walk outside and carry your skis to the snow.

The easiest way to carry yer skis!

- ~ Step SIX: Put the skis on.

IN THE PARKING LOT

Each step represents a significant challenge for a young beginner skier. Things will always take longer than you expect, so plan ahead on these first days and show up a little bit early. By taking your time, your little skier will be learning and having fun at each step.

Set yourself up for success. Your goal should be to *have fun*, and this means reducing (or eliminating) any stress ahead of time. There is an awful lot of stuff to organize and make happen before the skiing actually starts. Be careful, the buildup and the pressure to perform can create unrealistic expectations.

Arriving at the base area

If you can, drop off an adult and the kids right up close to the lodge. Unload only the gear they'll need while the driver parks the car. Kids should walk in their regular shoes, and then change into ski boots in the lodge.

Parents can use a huge duffel bag to hold all the kids' gear; then they can more easily carry it from the car to the lodge. Some people like to put the bag and ski gear on a cheap plastic sled and pull it that way.

Staying organized is a skill

There are a lot of items required for skiing. Role model that being a skier means taking care of your gear. This simple bit of awareness helps develop an overall sense of responsibility and respect for the mountain and other skiers. It's important that children learn how to carry their own gear, how to set their skis out on level terrain, and how to put them on a rack or out of the way at a break so they don't get lost or cause a mess for other skiers. Run through a checklist with your child. This will remind both of you to stay organized.

Stay organized by making good use of cubbies in the lodge.

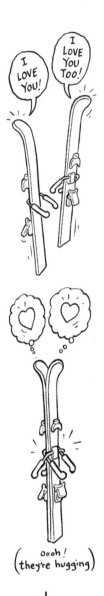

(I LOVE YOU!)
(I LOVE YOU TOO!)

oooh!
(they're hugging)

the
BRAKES
can
clip the
skis
together!

In the lodge

The process of putting the boots on should begin with the children sitting on a bench or chair. This makes it easy to pull off their street shoes, pull up ski socks, and smooth out long underwear cuffs. Usually, they'll put their toes into the boot while you hold it open, and then they'll stand up and use their own weight to slide their foot all the way into the boot. You need to be down on your knees guiding the process.

Thinner socks are preferred over thicker ones. Warmth is less the issue than the control they'll get from the better fit. The socks should be tall enough to come up well over the boots, and they should be pulled up snug so they are nice and smooth before the boot goes on.

Make sure to check in about the boots a few times during the day. Sometimes they might require a little maintenance. It's easiest to get down on your knees when adjusting the children's buckles (tightening or loosening); each time you check make sure the socks are pulled up nice and tall.

Each time you put the boots on, or adjust them, make sure to ask: Are your boots too tight? Can you wiggle your toes? Are your feet warm? Do both boots feel the same? Give them time to answer, walk around a little, and ask again.

For first-time never-ever skiers, make sure the boots are fitted for comfort and warmth. As they move into more difficult terrain, they'll need to make the boots a bit more snug for more control over the skis.

Checklist anytime you ski with kids

~ Have fun
~ Be patient
~ Play games
~ Practice
~ Try something new
~ Take breaks
~ Carry snacks

Plan ahead for the end of the day

Make sure to wrap up the day well before your young skier is out of energy. The most challenging runs of the day should happen early on, after a good warm-up. End the day with some easy, fun runs. They'll still need energy to change boots, organize all the gear, and get headed for home. Better to end early with a happy kid than late with them feeling miserable.

Make sure to have some warm, dry clothes ready to change into at the end of the day. This is easier in the lodge than in the parking lot. Change from ski boots to shoes. Dry socks can change anyone's mood!

Take some time for review and reflection. Kids love to retell the story of the day. Where did we go? What did we see? What did we learn how to do? This process will help them form a memory and story of a great day. By asking questions—what will we do next time? what are we working on?—you'll set the groundwork for the next skiing adventure.

HAT

NECK GAITER

MITTENS

use yer **HELMET** like a bucket to organize yer gear

PUT STUFF INSIDE DURING BREAKS

FLIP yer **HELMET** OVER so it doesn't roll away!

Practice FIRST without your skis and only your boots!

LEANING FORWARD — Stable

LEANING BACKWARD — awkward

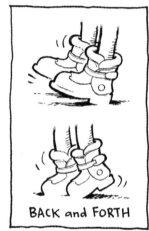

BACK and FORTH

SIDE to SIDE

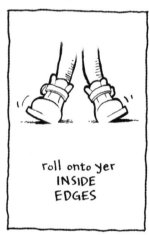

roll onto yer INSIDE EDGES

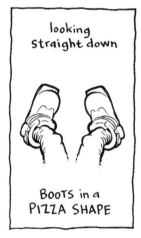

looking straight down

BOOTS in a PIZZA SHAPE

balance on ONE BOOT

CLOSE UP

BOW-TIE

TWIST YER BOOT

MAKE a BOW-TIE SHAPE

All these simple concepts transfer to the skills needed for skiing!

FIRST TIME EVER ON SKIS

The super basics

This initial run-through doesn't have to be at a ski area. You can have fun and introduce the simplest techniques in your backyard or on an open little hill in your neighborhood. Plastic strap-on skis might be fine here.

If you are at a ski area, start any first-time skiers in an open flat area and make sure there are no oncoming skiers or unwelcome traffic. You don't want any additional stresses or distractions. Start with the absolute basics.

Set your skis aside and focus on the new feelings that come with stiff ski boots. Move around on the snow. Try some silly walks. Clomp like Frankenstein. Hop like a bunny and walk sideways. Try jumping and landing on both feet.

Have the kids look down at their boots; they should be about as wide as their shoulders. This is a balanced stance, and they'll use this when they ski. Show the athletic pose, knees bent, leaning your shins into the tongue of the boot and hands out front.

Now have them balance on their toes and push their heels apart; their toes should be pointing toward each other. Look at

LEAN FORWARD and PRESS your SHINS against the TONGUE of the boot

AWESOME STANCE!

the shape that makes. It looks kinda like a slice of pizza, right? Get down on the snow and trace that shape with your fingers so the little one can visualize it. Explain that when you get your skis on, you're gonna use this triangle Pizza shape to stop.

Next, grab one ski. Check it out. Where's the front? Where's the back? Where's your foot go? How's your foot go into it? Let's put just one ski on. Whoa, it's slippery! But not too bad with one foot on the snow. Shuffle around. Try to scooter along and glide a little. Try to stand in one place and turn in a circle, you'll need to make tiny movements. Tip leg and knee in, and check out how that makes the inside edge *grab*, *slice*, and *bite* the snow.

Putting on the skis

Don't underestimate this simple task. It can take a lot longer than you think! Children will be dealing with technology they have never seen before, and they'll be excited and overwhelmed by everything around them.

With their baggy clothes they might not even be able to see their own feet, so you'll need to guide them through the process.

TAP the **SNOW OFF** THE BOTTOM of yer **BOOT** using the FRONT TOE part of the binding

STICKY SNOW

MAKE SURE THE HEEL IS DOWN!

~ Find a flat compacted zone of snow away from the hubbub. Line up the skis on the snow perpendicular to the fall line so they won't slide downhill.

~ Get down on your knees on the snow.

~ Make sure the heel of the binding is positioned "down" so it is ready to receive the child's boot.

~ Make sure there is no sticky snow stuck on the bottom of the boot. If there is, peel it off with your hands or tap it off on the front toe part of the binding.

~ Use your hands and position the toe into the boot with the front of the boot pointing down.

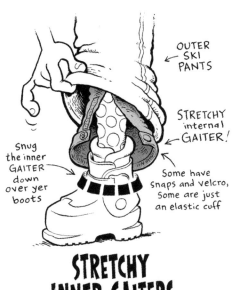

OUTER
SKI
PANTS

STRETCHY
internal
GAITER!

Snug
the inner
GAITER
down
over yer
boots

Some have
snaps and velcro,
some are just
an elastic cuff

STRETCHY INNER GAITERS

(hidden in yer ski pants)

~ Use your hands and position the heel into the back part of the binding.

~ Ask the child to lean back a little and step down.

~ Repeat these steps for the other foot.

~ Be patient. Good coaching early on will enable them to do it on their own before you know it.

THE TOE
GOES IN
FIRST

GET RIGHT
DOWN
ON THE
SNOW

MAKE SURE
THE HEEL
IS
DOWN!

HELPING to PUT the SKIS ON

KEEP THE POINTY PART away from the CHILD

Moving with skis on flat terrain

Ready for both skis? Do all the same stuff. They're like giant shoes! Watch out, don't cross your skis and don't step on your feet or you'll fall. Ask them to slide the skis back and forth and feel how slippery they are underneath. Suggest that they turn all the way around little by little. Show them how to use tiny motions. Just play with moving around with these long slippery skis. Shuffle and take little steps. Try to shuffle forward *without* lifting your skis off the snow.

Show them how a gentle slope works, how you stay in place when you are on the flattest areas, and how you glide with even a little bit of a slope. Sometimes you can even glide backward!

Try to make a wedge shape (Pizza) with both skis. You can draw the shape in the snow for them to see. Point your toes and the tips of your skis at each other. Now, bend both knees toward each other. This is how to stop on the hill. Rotate both feet to make the wedge shape.

Show them how to edge by angling their shins and pointing with their knees. They'll see (and feel) how the edges bite into the snow.

tiny steps...

EASY

Sized for a mouse

stomping a STAIRCASE in the snow

SIDE STEPPING

Taking the skis off

Kids can bend over a little easier than adults, so they might be able to reach down and push the back of the binding with their own hands. Encourage them to try.

~ They'll need assistance the first few times, and it really helps to get out of your skis so you can get in close.

~ You can give them a hand for balance and then push their heel tab down for them with your boot.

~ After a few times, encourage them to get out of the other ski themselves; they can use the tail of their own ski and boot to push down the heel tab on the opposite binding.

~ Don't just let the skis lie there, set them against something (they may be too short for the ski rack) or push the tails into the snow so they stand upright by themselves.

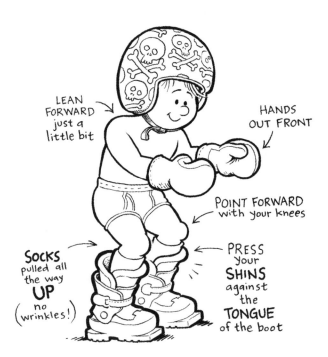

LEAN FORWARD just a little bit

HANDS OUT FRONT

POINT FORWARD with your knees

SOCKS pulled all the way UP (no wrinkles!)

PRESS your SHINS against the TONGUE of the boot

THE SKIER'S STANCE

A NICE PRACTICE SLOPE

Find a spot to practice on a beginner's hill
that transitions into a gentle uphill so you'll stop!

The very first time gliding downhill

Any ski area will have a super-mellow slope as part of the beginner terrain. Pick a spot with a nice flat runout so they'll stop all by themselves. As the adult, you probably won't need your skis. Just walking along with them is fine at first.

~ Simply work on gliding straight down this easy slope. Balancing while moving is a new sensation.

~ Coach and demonstrate a balanced stance, with hands out front and your feet as wide as your shoulders.

~ Practice, practice, practice. As your beginner gets more comfortable, start them up a little higher up the hill.

~ Once they're comfortable with gliding, use that same mellow slope to try the wedge or Pizza. At first the Pizza will be used simply for slowing down and stopping (*lotsa Pizza info comin' up next*). It's important to nail down the super basics before heading to the magic carpet.

~ The youngest first-timers often don't have enough leg strength or coordination to keep their skis in the Pizza shape. The Edgie-Wedgie (covered in the next chapter) can be a big help with these little skiers.

THE PIZZA

DRAW A PIZZA SHAPE
IN THE SNOW

Starting with the wedge

The pizza slice–shaped wedge is the foundation of speed control, turning, and stopping for the beginner skier. Just saying *make a Pizza shape with your skis* might not be enough. Draw the Pizza shape in the snow so the kids can look right at a tidy visual.

nice!

KNEES TILTED TOWARD EACH OTHER

The inside **SKI EDGES** are pushed into the SNOW

you should be able to fit a hand **UNDER** the outside edge of the SKIS

Get down in front and hold the ski tips and ask your little skiers to push their heels apart. With the tips held in place, the tails will slide out wide and the children will have created the triangle Pizza shape with their skis. Have a look at where the skis meet the snow. If the bottoms of their skis are flat on the snow, they will be ready to glide away. They'll need to slow down and stop by getting their edges to bite into the snow.

You can help them tip their edges into the snow by easing their knees and shins inside a little so the outside edges tip up a little bit. If you need to, reach right in there and position their boots to create the skiers' wedge; think of a boat with a curved hull starting from the bow.

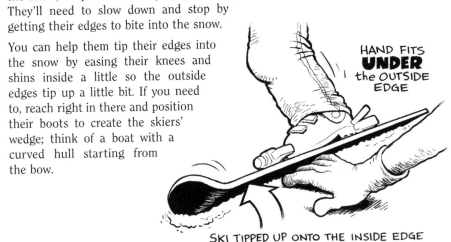

HAND FITS **UNDER** the OUTSIDE EDGE

SKI TIPPED UP ONTO THE INSIDE EDGE

The Pizza

GOOD PIZZA STANCE
(and where to press yer shins)

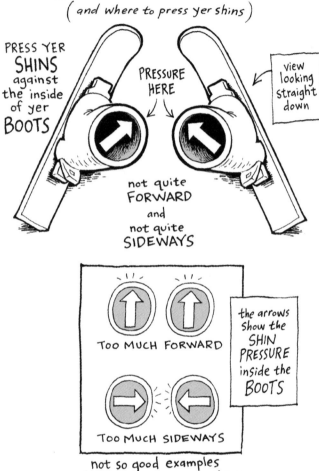

PRESS YER **SHINS** against the inside of yer **BOOTS**

PRESSURE HERE

view looking straight down

not quite FORWARD and not quite SIDEWAYS

TOO MUCH FORWARD

TOO MUCH SIDEWAYS

the arrows show the **SHIN PRESSURE** inside the **BOOTS**

not so good examples of where to press yer shins

Work together and get the inside edges tipped down into the snow. There will be a little space between the base of the ski and snow. You can check this by slipping your hand under the outside edge of the ski. Once they get it, they can hold themselves still even when pointed downhill.

Let 'em slide downhill and encourage them to go slow by using their edges. Make sure any beginner has a pretty good handle on the Pizza *before* venturing onto the magic carpet.

PIZZA
and the
TRACKS IN THE SNOW

NICE SIZED PIZZA SLICE!
(Not too wide)

HUGE PIZZA SLICE!
(Yikes! Too BIG!)

WHY CAN'T I STOP?

KNEES ARE **TOO FAR** APART

SKIS ARE **TOO FLAT** on the snow!
(that means the edges won't BITE the snow to slow you down)

EDGIE WEDGIE
(in use)

nice
PIZZA
shaped
wedge

Edgie Wedgie

This simple little device is super helpful for the first-time never-ever skiers and the youngest skiers. It's a great confidence builder and stepping stone tool for these little folks. The Edgie Wedgie attaches to both skis and keeps beginner's skis from separating. Position the thumb screw on the bottom of the ski and slightly down the inside from the tip.

The Edgie Wedgie can really help the youngest beginners feel more comfortable on their skis by keeping those ski tips from spreading out. The little tool forms a nice Pizza wedge so they can more easily control their speed. This can be a real confidence booster for the never-evers or children who are so young that they just don't have the required muscle strength or coordination to hold their skis in a wedge without some help. The Edgie Wedgie enables children to focus on core skills like balancing while their feet stay in the wedge position.

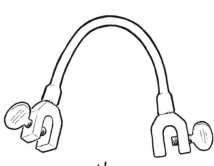

the
EDGIE WEDGIE!

TIE an
overhand
KNOT

if y'need
to shorten

The Pizza   **39**

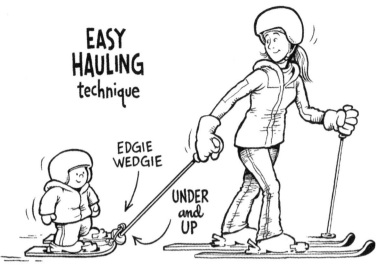

EASY HAULING technique

EDGIE WEDGIE

UNDER and UP

EDGIE WEDGIE
as a two-headed worm!

mmm...

Edgie Wedgie
(in use)

CHOMP!

Put both ends on
one ski tip
for shuffling
on the flats
and
the magic carpet!

Even if you are teaching children who have moved past using the Edgie Wedgie, you might want to keep one in your pocket. It may only get used on that last run of the day when they are feeling tired and can't hold the wedge anymore. It only takes a few seconds to put it on their skis, and it might make everyone's day end on a high note.

Sometimes the cord on the Edgie Wedgie is too long, especially for the tiniest skiers. A simple solution is to just tie an overhand knot in the cord. Easy!

You might wanna try putting the Edgie Wedgie on your own skis to see how it helps hold the Pizza shape. You'll also realize that it makes it almost impossible to shuffle on the flats! If your child has an Edgie Wedgie in place, you'll need to help them on flat terrain by holding their hand (and pulling them) or by quickly bending down and just undoing one side.

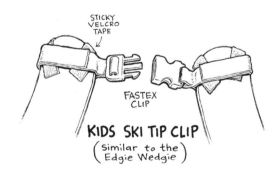

STICKY VELCRO TAPE

FASTEX CLIP

KIDS SKI TIP CLIP
(Similar to the)
(Edgie Wedgie)

THE BASIC SKILLS

The magic carpet

The magic carpet is a very simple conveyor belt that brings skiers up to the top of the beginners' slope. These have replaced the tow-ropes from a bygone era. They don't require much instruction; you just give the person ahead the right amount of space and then shuffle on the track. Then, you just stand there until you get to the top.

There will be an attendant at the top who is used to helping kids get off and to the side. They'll need to keep moving after they get off the moving carpet. They should shuffle off to the side so the other skiers have some room when they arrive in the unloading spot.

WEDGE CHRISTIE

Use the magic carpet as a tool for teaching the basic skills required for safety: turning and stopping. Have fun on the mellowest slope. Practice the foundations. There is no hurry (and no pressure) to move onto the chairlift. That's a huge step and rushing into that realm will work against you.

HELPFUL ATTENDANT

AMAZING X-RAY VIEW

SECRET POWER SOURCE UNDER THE SNOW!

THE MAGIC CARPET

Stopping

Games make everything more fun! For stopping, play Red Light, Green Light! Stand a little bit below the skiers on a smooth straight run. Have them parked in a wedge pointed downhill. When you say "Green Light," they can go. Let 'em glide in a wedge for 10 feet or so, then call out "Red Light." They should stop as quickly as they can. You can add "Yellow Light" for slowing down.

Coach them though the challenges. Maybe their Pizza isn't big enough to stop, or it's too big to go. Have them focus on pushing their heels apart. Sometimes the Pizza is big enough, but the edges aren't biting the snow. Have them ease their knees a little closer together as a way to get the skis to roll onto the inside edges. High fives all around when they can stop and go on a dime.

Show them that simply sitting down in a controlled plop is an easy way to stop. If they look like they are out of control, hollering *"sit down!"* may be more useful than *"stop!"*

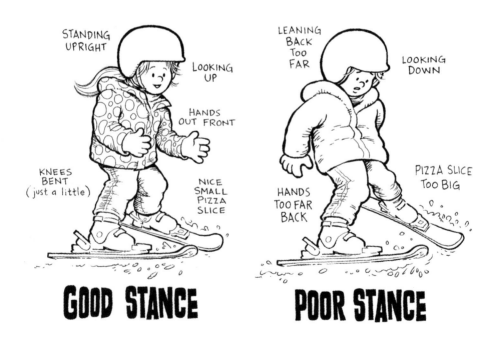

STANDING UPRIGHT

LOOKING UP

HANDS OUT FRONT

KNEES BENT (just a little)

NICE SMALL PIZZA SLICE

GOOD STANCE

LEANING BACK TOO FAR

LOOKING DOWN

HANDS TOO FAR BACK

PIZZA SLICE TOO BIG

POOR STANCE

PRACTICE SKIING AROUND OBSTACLES

AWESOME!

RIGHT ON FOR ME!

MOST SKI SCHOOLS and BEGINNER SLOPES WILL HAVE HANDY PROPS, LIKE PYLONS

WEDGE CHRISTIE

Turning

Next introduce turning (lots more on this to come). Basic turning means putting more pressure on one ski than the other. Start with turning to one side. Draw a big arcing C shape in the snow. Start in a wedge; ask them to put most of their weight on one ski and keep it there while you all count to "Three Mississippi" as your little skiers slide. In most cases they will make a nice, easy turn to one side. If not, you may need to coach them to keep weight on one ski, or to make sure that the edge on that ski is biting the snow, roll the pressured knee inward.

Practice single turns on both sides. Once that is easy, try linking turns. Draw a big S in the snow. Coach them through the transitions by pointing and calling out: "Stand on that leg! Now stand on that leg!" back and forth as they connect turns.

Some beginner slopes will have helpful props available, like little orange cones and hula hoops. If they don't, you can be creative and have them ski around you!

It might not take long before they'll be ready for the chairlift. Depending on their age and how quickly they master the basic skills, some kids may only do a few runs on the magic carpet before they graduate to the chairlift. Others (especially the youngest) may need a few days.

You can move on to the chairlift once the little skiers can consistently control their speed by turning and stopping. No need to hurry off the magic carpet. If it's fun, then keep at it. Practice, practice, practice (and play, play, play!) before moving on.

Hula hoop

One of the simplest (and most fun) tools is a hula hoop! Sometimes the ski instructors keep a stash of hula hoops near the beginner slopes. They are light and springy and you can use 'em to slow the kids down, or they can hold on if you need to drag them uphill a short ways.

The hula hoop isn't required; kids can learn just fine without it. But it can be a fun tool that will give parents a little peace of mind for kid wrangling on the slopes.

Helping 'em up after they fall

For brand new little skiers, the teacher should be helping 'em get up after falling. For the youngest skiers, just pick 'em up when they plop over. The initial goal is just to get lots of practice sliding: no need to add the frustrations of learning to get up on their own. That'll come soon enough. At first it's much easier if the teacher isn't wearing skis. Just pick the kids up and put them down so their skis are *sideways* to the fall line or in a solid Pizza wedge. Make sure they are balanced and edged before letting go. If the teacher is wearing skis (and short skis are better), position yourself sideways and below the kids before lifting 'em up.

Get in close and de-tangle the wreck

Encourage 'em to kick their skis downhill

Encourage 'em to get up onto their side

Get in close and help 'em up!

HELPING 'EM
to get up on their own

MOVING TO THE GREENS

LOOK UPHILL

Big slope safety

Moving to the chairlift on the bigger slopes is a big deal. You'll be entering a new realm with new challenges. Skiing has its hazards, but almost all accidents can be prevented with an attitude of caution and awareness.

Some kids are totally fearless even if it's their first time ever on skis! There is a certain breed that will ignore the whole speed control idea and just point 'em down and let 'em rip. This can be kinda scary if you're on a crowded slope, with other skiers, trees, and lift towers. Catching a little runaway takes determination, so it's better to prevent any of these issues ahead of time. Safe skiing is everyone's responsibility, regardless of your abilities. Teach your children the benefits of being courteous and aware of the other skiers—and model this yourself too.

Skier's responsibility code

The National Ski Areas Association, the National Ski Patrol, and the Professional Ski Instructors Association officially endorsed the Skier's Responsibility Code:

~ Always stay in control! This means you must be able to stop or avoid other people or objects.

~ People ahead of you have the right of way. It is your responsibility to avoid them, not for them to avoid you!

~ You must not stop where you obstruct a trail, or are not visible from above. You'll need to role model this with kids, showing them how to get to the side of a run. Ski with them to the side and explain why you are stopping there.

~ Whenever starting downhill or merging into a trail, look uphill first and yield to others.

~ Always use devices to help prevent runaway equipment, like a ski leash or ski brakes.

~ Observe all the posted signs and warnings. Keep off closed trails and out of closed areas.

~ Before you get on any lift, you must have the knowledge and ability to load, ride, and unload safely.

This list is taken very seriously at each and every ski resort. These tips aren't complicated; they are just common sense and courtesy.

Safety and getting on and off the chairlift

The first chairlift ride is a huge step. You are taking a little child on something suspended way up in the air, so safety precautions need to be taken seriously. Here's a list of points that will help make that first ride go smoothly.

You can practice getting on the chairlift using a bench

~ Preview the whole thing. Find a place where you can watch how other people get on the chairlift. Point out everything, talk about it.

~Parents and teachers should leave their poles behind–they'll only be a nuisance.

~ Get all organized in the line.

NEXT LIFT LOAD OF SKIERS WAITING

the WAIT HERE LINE

MOVE QUICKLY!

the LIFTIE

the STAND HERE LINE

~ Talk to the lift attendant (lovingly known as the *liftie*). Make sure to tell him that this is the child's first ever chairlift ride. Ask if he can slow the chair down.

~ Sandwich the kids between two adults, or position the kids on the outside of the chair near the liftie. The attendants at any "Green" lift will be accustomed to boosting kids onto the chair. But they can only do this with the kids closest to them. Kids who are in the middle of the chair won't get a liftie boost.

~ Everybody lines up at the "wait here" line (*the starting gate!*). Don't go over the line or the chair might bump you as it swings around. Each person gets their own lane. Watch the chair ahead of you as it passes by.

~ Chase the chair after it goes by, shuffle forward. Stay in your lane! You might need to do some pushing and pulling to get 'em moving fast enough.

~ Line your boots up at the next line.

~ Everybody turns around and watches the approaching chair.

~ How much help you give them depends on their size and comfort.

LIFT ATTENDANT

LIFTIE

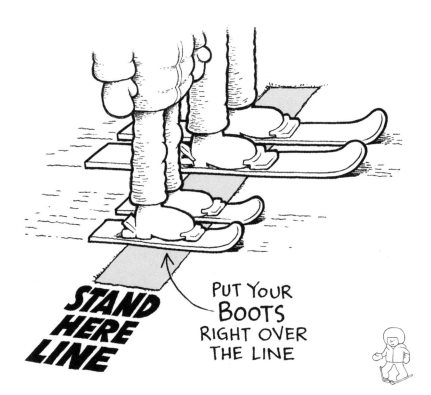

STAND HERE LINE

PUT YOUR
BOOTS
RIGHT OVER
THE LINE

It's normal to just pick up the smaller kids and set them on the chair. It's best if they do most of the work, but that might not happen until they are bigger or have more practice.

~ You sit down just a micro-second after them.

~ Once you are on, slide 'em back away from the edge. Keep your arm in front of them. If there is a safety bar, put it down.

~ Sit still on the ride and no slouching!

I need
some help

BUTT BELOW

← Stand "HERE" line

KIDS with BUTTS
below the
height of the chair
will need help getting on...

Easy...

BUTT ABOVE

← Stand "HERE" line

Moving to the Greens

LIFTING TIP FOR THE KIDS
who need help getting up onto the chairlift

KEEP EVERYONE'S SKIS STRAIGHT!

it helps to practice beforehand using a bench

The liftie can help boost kids into the chair

REMEMBER
ALWAYS
PUT
DOWN
the
SAFETY
BAR!

Mistakes getting on the chairlift

Don't lift the children into your own lap; they need to end up sitting on the chair, facing forward, all by themselves. *And don't try this with poles!*

Preview the world of the big slope

While riding on the chairlift, you'll have an awesome view of the brand new run that you'll soon be skiing on. Point out the big features, like where trails merge and turns in the run. This can be a time to preview what's coming up next on the slopes below.

After you're all successfully off the chair, pull over to the side where you are out of the way and can watch the chairs behind you as skiers unload. Reviewing this will help your child understand better what's going on and make next time easier!

UPPER LEGS ARE TOO SHORT!

a little bit more secure!

SAFE POSITION SITTING ON THE CHAIRLIFT
for the smallest kids

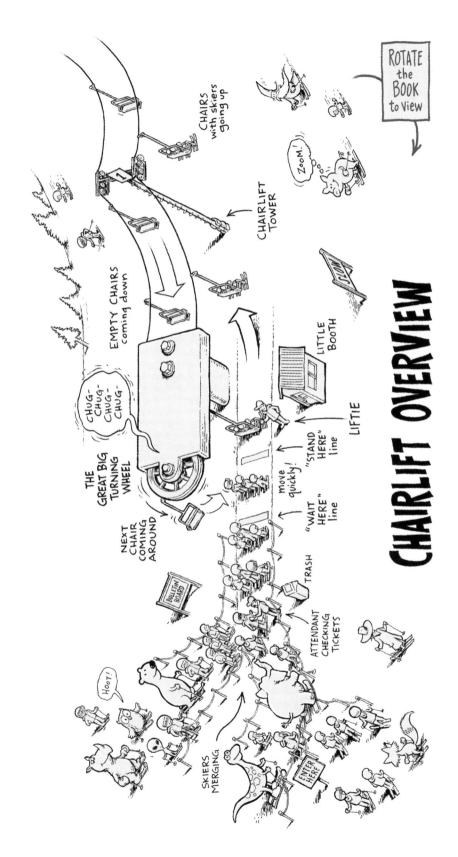

Getting off the chairlift

~ While you are on the chair, make a plan before you get to the top. Which way are we going? Review these steps: Ski tips up as you approach, no need to jump, *just stand up*, keep the skis pointing straight when you stand up, and ski faster than the chair.

~ Make a plan on where to move after sliding down the ramp. Point to something rather than saying right or left.

~ Explain that you'll have your hand in the small of their back to help them if they need it. Put your hand there so they know how it feels.

~ Sometimes you can signal the up-top liftie to slow the chair down for off-loading. If they see someone with a child making the universal gesture for "slow down," they'll know what to do.

~ Let them help lift the bar, but don't let them scoot too close to the edge of the chair.

~ Put your hand behind them, low in the small of their back.

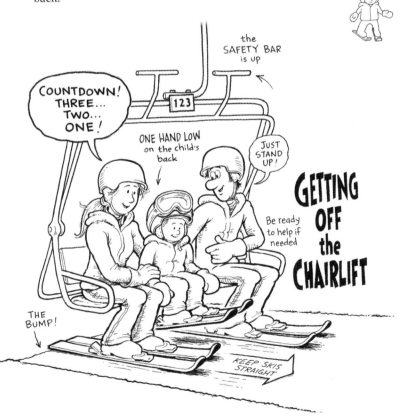

~ Do a countdown and involve the children: *"Get ready! Five - Four - Ski tips up - Three . . ."*

~ Everybody lifts their ski tips up as you approach the platform.

~ *". . .Two - ONE - Stand up!"* Everybody stands up at the same time. All the children really need to do is stand, and you can guide them forward with your hand low on their back. Let them stand up on their own. Even though it's tempting, don't hold them under their armpits and hoist them off the chair.

~ Children who are so tiny their feet cannot reach the snow will need to jump instead of simply standing up. Guide them rather than lifting them and setting them down. If the children cling on to you, or if you try to reach sideways and lift them, they might end up on the platform standing with their skis pointing sideways instead of straight ahead.

~ After they are standing, encourage them to shuffle forward; gently push them if they need it. French Fries only for sliding down the ramp.

~ Ease them down the ramp and quickly move them off to the side and out of the way.

EASY GREENS

Checklist for the easiest Green runs

~ Take time to point out all the features of *The Big Hill*

~ Talk about how to be safe

~ Practice in wide open areas

~ Work on skills while moving nice and slow

~ Try different-size turns

~ Follow the leader

~ Play balancing games

~ Work on getting up without help

~ Introduce good habits

~ Practice

~ Have fun

~ Go in, get warm, drink hot chocolate

No need to push your knees together to make a PIZZA shape...

nice PIZZA KNEES (gotta have 'em!)

good PIZZA stance!

The fall line

Every skier knows the term *the fall line*. This is the imaginary line that a big beach ball would take if it was rolling down the ski slope. If you just point your skis downhill while skiing, *you'll zoom way too fast!* Skiing requires speed control, and that means turning.

The ball only wants to go one way: It wants to follow the path of least resistance and the pull of gravity. Obviously, if you pointed your skis straight down the hill, right into the fall line (or the *gravity* line), you would end up zooming really fast. The easiest way to slow down would be to turn *out* of this invisible line and go sideways along the slope. The best way to show this is standing at the top of a long run and looking downhill.

This term might be too complicated for a young learner. Instead of trying to teach the idea of the fall line, better to simply say the *go line* to *go fast*, and the *slow line* to *go slow*.

When it comes time to practice with the youngest learners, it's easier for them if you are super literal. You can show it to them by skiing out in front and telling them to follow in your tracks. It's easy to demonstrate the difference between *go* and *slow*.

You can also point to something on the side of the slope and say, "Ski to that tree and watch how slow and in control you are."

THE FALL LINE
this is the line
where a
BIG BEACH BALL
WOULD ROLL
DOWNHILL
~also called~
THE GO LINE!

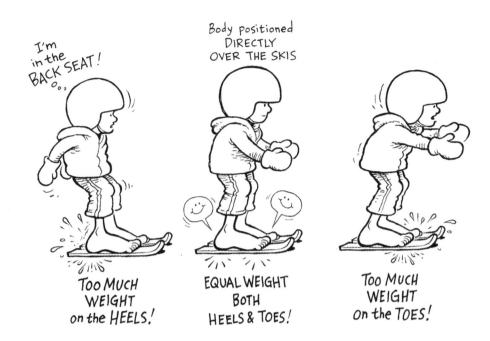

TOO MUCH WEIGHT on the HEELS!

EQUAL WEIGHT BOTH HEELS & TOES!

TOO MUCH WEIGHT On the TOES!

Stay out of the back seat!

As you ski, the weight of your body should fall between your heel and toe. It will move toward your toes or toward your heel depending on where you are in your turn or if you hit some unexpected bumps. The important thing is to *keep your weight between your heel and toe.* Be aware that boots for kids are tall and stiff when compared to their tiny and super-flexible ankles, so it's easy for 'em to lean backward and rest against the back of the boot. They can actually ski like this, but this *back seat* pose makes it really hard to make your skis work, so they won't be able to turn or stop correctly. Remember that the steering wheel of the skis is up front.

Make sure new skiers understand that they have to balance between heel and toe. They probably won't tip over if they lean too far back, but they won't be able to truly control their skis in that pose.

LEANING BACK TOO FAR!

THE BACK SEAT

PRETEND you're holding a STEERING WHEEL

GOOD BODY POSITION!

This keeps your HANDS FOREWARD in front of you

Keep your hands out front!

To keep your little skier in balance, coach them to keep their hands out in front of 'em, rather than down at their sides (or worse, behind them). Being in balance means staying nice and stable right over the middle of your feet. If your hands slip down by your pockets or behind you, then you're in the *back seat!* This means you are leaning too far back on your heels and your leg is pushing against the back of your boot. Just imagine your hands on a steering wheel to keep you in the perfect skier's pose!

An easy way to work on this skill is for you as the teacher to ski backward just a little ways in front of the skiers. You'll position your hands facing upward while they keep their hands hovering over yours facing downward. Try not to touch each other. This will require a little concentration, and the children will need to keep their eyes focused on your hands. This keeps 'em looking forward and up. If they do falter, you can easily grab their hands and support them.

HOLD A **SNOWBALL** and **PRETEND** IT'S A **DINOSAUR EGG!**

KEEP IT STEADY!

HANDS OUT FRONT!

Another easy game is to make a big snowball and try to carry it out front with both hands. Pretend it's a fragile dinosaur egg, so don't drop it! Can you carry it all the way to the bottom of the run?

The opposite of good hand positions is when arms are flailing around trying to keep the little skier in balance. This awkward motion is called *spaghetti arms*.

One easy thing you can do to fix the dreaded spaghetti arms is to clap your hands (nice and loud) any time you feel even a little bit out of balance. This forces both hands out front in the perfect position.

SPAGHETTI ARMS
(clumsy, awkward, and crummy style)

Look up!

It's normal for children to look down at their own skis while gliding downhill. This is a problem with adults too, but because children's heads are larger in proportion to their bodies, for kids it can create a really awkward stance on the skis. An easy way to solve this is to ski a little ways in front of them, and ask them to watch your hands. Move nice and slow and ask them to call out how many fingers you are showing. Mittens make this game tricky, so it might just be *thumbs up* and *thumbs down*.

slipping off balance!

ZAPPED BACK INTO PERFECT BODY POSITION!

if you slip off balance...
CLAP YOUR HANDS!

FRENCH FRIES

PUT YER HANDS OVER EACH OTHER, But don't touch!

BE CAREFUL! DON'T RUN INTO SKIERS BEHIND YOU!

LOOKING FORWARD

ARMS OUT FRONT

SKIING BACKWARD

Carry a toy!

If you are playing the role of instructor, you might wanna carry a little stuffed animal as part of your overall teaching strategy. It needs to be small enough that it fits in your pocket, but big enough that it's easy for kids to grab off the snow with mittens. By skiing in front of the kids and getting them to focus on the stuffed animal, you can teach them to look up. A funny hand puppet is great for this too!

Follow the leader

This is an easy way to get focused on turning. Get a little bit out in front of them and tell them to follow in your tracks. You play the engine and the child is the caboose. You can teach them the go line and the slow line (see illustration on page 57) by going faster straight down the fall line and going slower across the fall line.

You can stop and start by calling out "red light" and "green light." This is a little more fun than yelling "stop" or "start," which can sound a little harsh. You can add "yellow light" for slowing down.

Don't get too far in front of your children. If they fall and need help, you'll want to be close by so you won't need to hike a long way back up the hill.

Falling down and getting up

When new skiers fall and need help getting up, just ski right up close (wearing short skis in the role of teacher helps a lot) and lift 'em upright again. Make sure to position them with their skis *across* the fall line.

If they need your assistance, give it to 'em. While you are helping them back up, make sure to praise them. "You did great!" and "It's okay to fall!" are what they need to hear. An "I'm proud of you for trying so hard" never hurts either!

There will come a point when they'll need to get up on their own, and every child has a different level of independence. Pretend that you've just fallen down, so you'll be down on the snow right next to them. Then show them the steps for getting up. You can do it together.

Getting up on their own

Anyone who falls, big or small, needs to first get their feet (and both skis) *downhill* below their body and positioned *across* the fall line. This simple technique is second nature to anyone with even a tiny bit of skiing experience. But it can be confusing to a child, they might be uncertain how to position their skis while they are lying in the snow.

At first just get in close and reach down and position their body and skis so they are set up for success.

Getting them to start by rolling over onto their back is easiest. Then they can twirl their skis below their body and position them so their feet are downhill. This might be tricky because the slope is going to be very slight, so they might not be able to visualize where downhill really is.

The next step is to get them into a body position where they can actually get up all by themselves. One simple trick is to draw a curving rainbow in the snow with your finger, connecting their knees to the tips of their skis. You should draw this for them at first, and after they've seen you do it a few times you can encourage them to draw it themselves.

The next step is to have them walk their hands along that rainbow in the snow, starting at their knees and moving in the line toward their ski tips. You can panto-mime this with your own hands right in the rainbow. As they do it themselves, they'll get into a good body posi-tion as their palms near their tips, and they should be able to stand up all by themselves.

As you watch, you'll realize that their skis might not be positioned directly across the fall line, and they might start sliding forward or backward without knowing exactly why. As their coach, you'll need to be nice and close (and downhill) so you can save them from any unwanted sliding. When they are first learning this, just put your own ski or boot in front of or behind their skis (depending on which way they might slide) and then help them scooch their stance so they are in a nice stable pose with their skis across the fall line.

There are usually trees to the right and left of every slope. So an easy way to explain it (in a rhyme) is to say: Point your *skis* at the *trees*!

IF YOU ARE OUT OF CONTROL...

TOO FAST!

ZOOM!

PLOP!

I STOPPED!

...simply sitting down is a surefire way to STOP!

GETTING UP
(AFTER FALLING DOWN)

Pressure, edge, and steer!

These are the three basic ingredients for making a turn. For example, to turn left, you'll need to *pressure* (put more weight on) your right ski; once you've got that, lean that shin uphill so that ski can roll onto its inside *edge*. As it goes from flat to edged, it will start to bite and carve the snow; keep your weight on it and slowly *steer* the ski in the direction you want to go. This will work for wedge and parallel turns.

It's essential to *look in the new direction* of where you want to ski instead of looking down at the snow. *Look* where you want to *go!*

PUTTING **WEIGHT** on your downhill SKI will initiate the TURN

TAP the downhill THIGH

TAP the downhill THIGH

TAPPING your own DOWNHILL THIGH will remind you to **STRONGLY WEIGHT** that SKI!

Focus on the downhill leg

You gotta keep your weight on that downhill ski when turning. One way to stay focused on weighting your downhill ski is to tap on your downhill thigh with your hand. Halfway through the turn you'll need to *change sides* and start tapping the *other* thigh because it'll change to the *new* downhill ski.

Another good way to get your weight on your downhill ski is to imagine having one heavy elephant foot downhill and a skinny little featherweight bird leg for the uphill ski. These will switch back and forth as you change to the next turn.

HEAVY ELEPHANT FOOT!

FEATHER FOOT (light like a bird)

Lots more weight on the downhill ski!

Balance games

Skiing means balancing while in motion. These two tips will help you feel that magic balance point.

Try to hop while standing still. Jump straight up and try to land in a nice balanced pose. Next, try it while skiing forward. Try to take off and land and stay balanced the whole time. If you land on your heels you might slip like you just stepped on a banana peel!

For a good warm-up on cold days, think of the hops like popcorn popping. It starts slow and then the popping gets faster and faster.

Next, see if you can balance on one ski. First, try it standing still. Next, try it while skiing. Keep those hands forward and pressure that one foot between the toes and heel. How long can you hold it? One Mississippi? Two Mississippi? It's not as easy as it looks!

If you lift your uphill ski right off the snow you'll *know* that you are putting a lot of weight on your downhill ski! Find a gentle traverse and practice picking the uphill ski off the snow. Just an inch or two is plenty and it may only stay up for a few seconds. It's okay if the tip of the ski stays on the snow. If that happens, it shows that you've got great balance heel to toe and side to side! But, if the tip lifts up and the tail stays in the snow, you are leaning too far back.

TALL and SMALL picking flowers

TALL and SMALL for turns

Get **TALL** to start your turns. Standing up tall over the middle of the ski opens all the joints (ankles, knees, hips) and removes the pressure from the front and side of the boot. This will *release* your ski's edges from the snow and allow the ski to flatten and begin to turn downhill. Keep getting tall until you are in the go line and then get **SMALL** to shape the rounded end of the turn. Getting SMALL means bending at your ankles, knees, and hips so that you can guide the ski with finesse into the slow line to finish the turn.

Ski in front of the little ones so they can copy you. Call it out: "Get TALL!" That means hands over your head, reach for the clouds. "Get SMALL!" Hands low and out front, duck down low like you are skiing under a low branch!

You can "get SMALL" and pick flowers while turning. Flowers only grow on the outside of each turn. Then you can "get TALL" after the turn and add that flower to the bunch (with your hands out front) before scrunching down into the next turn.

Stay in a
GOOD STANCE
in both
TALL & SMALL

YER HEAD STAYS AT THE SAME LEVEL

TALL
EXTENSION

SMALL
COMPRESSION

TALL and SMALL for bumps

The TALL and SMALL technique helps you deal with bumpy terrain too. If you ski with your body all frozen up, then bumps and dips will throw you for a loop. Use TALL and SMALL movements to absorb the bumps as if your body is a shock absorber. Try skiing over a whoop-de-doo: *squash SMALL* over the top, and *extend TALL* in the valleys. Bumps and roly-polies can feel nice and smooth.

FRENCH FRIES

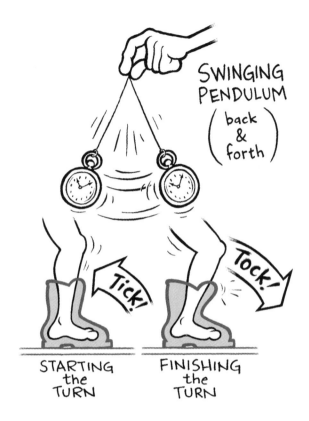

SWINGING PENDULUM
(back & forth)

Tick!

Tock!

STARTING the TURN

FINISHING the TURN

The swinging pendulum

When you ski, your knees and shins should move back and forth rhythmically like a swinging pendulum. Just like you did with TALL and SMALL, you'll need to open and close the ankle, knee, and hip joint to make this happen. The ankle opens for the top half of the turn. *Tick!* The ankle closes for the bottom half. *Tock!*

Make your movements as smooth as possible and, like the pendulum, keep moving. It's easy to get stuck and lose rhythm if the tic-tock stops. For long turns make a long *Tiiicccckkk* and a long *Toooccccckkk*. Short turns will sound much faster, *tick-tock-tick-tock-tick-tock*. Be careful not to hypnotize yourself with your rockin' steady rhythm.

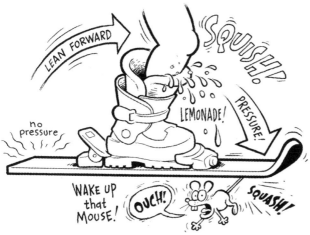

The juicer!

The boots are like a mechanical fruit juicer. Imagine putting your favorite fruit down between your shins and the front of the boot (the tongue). When they make turns they should be opening and closing the juicer, smashing your fruit into juice! Slowly open the juicer to release your edges and start the turn, slowly close the juicer to finish.

The faster you go with the juicer or the faster you get TALL and SMALL, the more turns you'll make. Big, slow turns will use the same movement, but in *slooowww* motion. It's fun to make different turn sizes. This is essential when the goal is to move on to harder runs.

(small) (TALL)

THE FIRST JUMP!

(keep yer knees a little bit bent)

NOT too big

Animal trails, roll-overs, jumps, and bumps

Don't just stay on the big open spaces; look for some more exciting terrain. Some ski resorts have a designated zone with props and kid-friendly trails designed for fun. Ask someone to point out the best places to take kids. You might find some downsized terrain park features sculpted specifically for young skiers: whoop-de-doos, roly-polies, banked turns, and giant croquet wickets!

Kids love animal trails. They can sneak in and out around trees, over humps, down chutes, and around banked corners. They emphasize balancing, braking, and turning moves. Make sure to stress safety. One at a time, leaving space between each skier, count to five heffalumps between skiers and stay in control! Be sure to teach your child to look for uphill skiers before they merge back onto the main trail!

These little trails are often rated for difficulty similar to the main runs. Start with the easiest and work your way up. Big people with long skis might find it hard to control their speed on little trails. Kids go first, adults follow (under control!) to pick up any crashes.

YIKES! too far back!

A CRUMMY LANDING

ouch!

MASTERING THE GREENS

SHORT STEEP SHOT!

FIND SOME SHORT ZONES of more CHALLENGING TERRAIN

with a

NICE FLAT RUNOUT!

Checklist for more challenging Green runs

~ Explore (this is an adventure!)

~ Add speed

~ Find rolls and bumps to practice balancing

~ Master getting up without help

~ Follow animal trails through the trees

~ Find short steep shots

~ Practice good habits

~ Keep hands balanced / hands downhill

~ Practice the Wedge Christie

~ Apply pressure on the outside foot or downhill foot

~ Polish the airplane turns

~ Work toward French Fries

~ Go in, get warm, drink hot chocolate

~ Have fun

NICE
FRENCH FRIES
(Nice and Straight)

French Fries skill builder

All skiers need plenty of practice with parallel skills *before* heading onto Blue terrain. They don't need to be skiing in perfect technique, but steeper slopes will require getting into a parallel, or *French Fries*, stance.

The next series of tips will lay the foundation for the parallel turn.

Terrain progression

Kids get the hang of skiing skills in subtle ways. Rather than trying to gauge their mastery of a bunch of specific skills, it might be easier to wrap your mind around how well they perform on different slopes of varying steepness and difficulty. Evaluate their progress by their comfort and finesse on varied terrain.

Make sure to teach and practice each skill on easy terrain *before* moving to more difficult slopes with more challenges and higher consequences. One of the worst mistakes you can make is pushing your child to more difficult terrain too quickly. Make sure they are both excited and ready to move on to the harder slope!

If you are going to try skiing on more challenging terrain, the child will be out of their comfort zone. Make sure to begin and end the day well within their comfort zone: no new challenges on steeper slopes on the first or last run of the day.

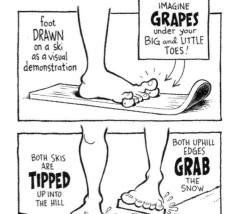

The mountain stance

This is a static pose on the slope. Just stand still with both skis in French Fries mode parallel to each other and perpendicular to the fall line. The trick is to roll both knees uphill so that the uphill pinkie toe and downhill big toe are in the snow.

THE ART of BIG TOE / LITTLE TOE
(with grapes!)

THE MOUNTAIN STANCE

Traversing in French Fries

Start in the mountain stance on an easy Green slope. Point your tips across the slope and a little bit downhill. Press your uphill pinkie toe into the snow as you move forward. This will keep that uphill, inside edge on the snow. If you do it right, you can look back and see two parallel sets of French Fries marked on the slope. Do it on both sides.

You should keep your body turned just a little bit downhill. Look in the direction you are skiing, but if you peek down at your skis as you traverse, you'll see the uphill ski is just a little bit forward. That means you're doing it right!

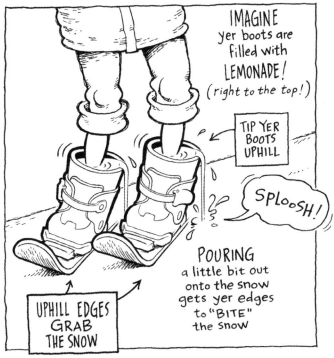

POUR YER DRINK!

(and edge yer skis)

Pour out a little drink

As you traverse a slope in French Fries mode, you'll need to keep those uphill edges biting into the snow. This means pointing your knees and shins a little uphill. A simple way to focus on those edges is to imagine your boots are filled with lemonade, right up to the very top. If you tip them a little, they'll *pour a drink* for the snow on the slope. They'll pour out exactly the same amount from both boots on the uphill side.

If your skis are slipping out of the traverse, this tip will help you get them to bite the snow and hold them on the slope. A friend can ski behind you and call out "pour a drink!" to help keep your skis in the stable French Fries pose.

Pizza and French Fries combo

In this exercise you'll ski on easy terrain alternating between the Pizza and French Fries technique. Find a nice gentle slope where you won't get going too fast. You might need to traverse a little sideways across the slope to stay in control for this one.

Don't worry about turning. Get going with a smooth gliding wedge. Stand up TALL and bring your skis together in parallel for One Mississippi, then get SMALL and sink back into your gliding wedge for One Mississippi. Transition back and forth between the Pizza and French Fries as smoothly as possible. Remember, no herky-jerky moves! You'll go a little faster when your skis are straight and parallel. And you'll slow down when your skis are in the wedge shape. Try to keep your speed even and transition with a nice steady rhythm.

You can combine this with the TALL and SMALL tip. Getting TALL allows you to flatten the skis and guide them together into French Fries. Getting SMALL enables you to gently tip the skis on edge so that you can make the Pizza wedge.

When you're done, check out the fat and skinny tracks! You should be able to see the skinny French Fries and the fat Pizza marks in the snow.

The Wedge Christie

This cool turn is the middle step between skiing in a Pizza wedge and skiing in French Fries. The goal is to use the stability of the Pizza (wedge) to start your turns and the efficiency of parallel skiing (French Fries) to shape and finish your turns.

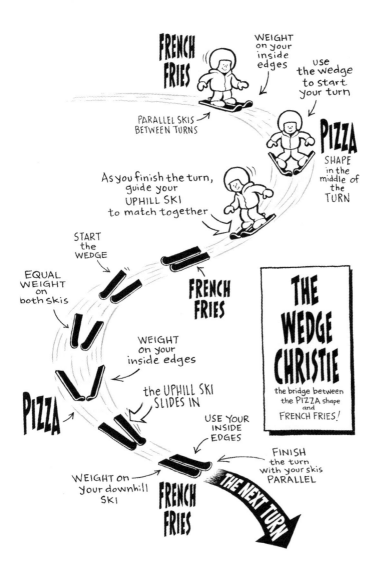

FRENCH FRIES

WEIGHT on your inside edges

use the wedge to start your turn

PARALLEL SKIS BETWEEN TURNS

PIZZA

SHAPE in the middle of the TURN

As you finish the turn, guide your UPHILL SKI to match together

START the WEDGE

EQUAL WEIGHT on both skis

FRENCH FRIES

WEIGHT on your inside edges

the UPHILL SKI SLIDES IN

PIZZA

USE YOUR INSIDE EDGES

WEIGHT on your downhill SKI

FRENCH FRIES

FINISH the turn with your skis PARALLEL

THE NEXT TURN

THE WEDGE CHRISTIE

the bridge between the PIZZA shape and FRENCH FRIES!

With a wedge turn, your balance is pretty much *centered* between your feet. This is very comfortable and stable. With a parallel turn, your balance will *pass over your feet* for a brief moment at the beginning of the turn.

Moving your balance across the skis at the start of the turn can feel a little scary. It's a lot like making that first turn on your bike without training wheels.

The Wedge Christie lets you keep the training wheels on for that tricky moment at the start of the turn. Use the Pizza as you get TALL and guide your skis into the go line, then get SMALL in the rounded bottom of the turn. Guide your uphill ski so it slides smoothly into French Fries.

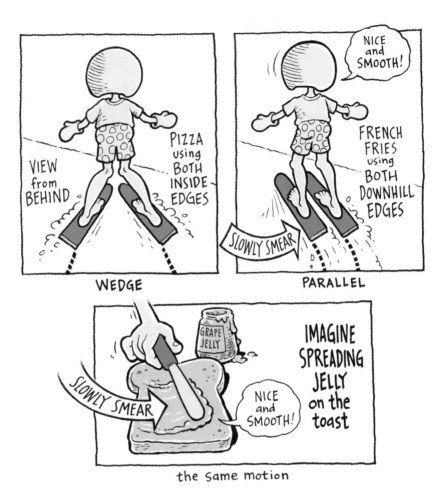

the same motion

MOVING FROM THE PIZZA TO THE FRENCH FRIES!

Think about guiding and *smearing* that uphill pinkie toe across the snow until the skis are parallel. If you are teaching, you can prompt this by calling out "*pinkie toe in the snow!*" (it rhymes!).

Imagine you are *spreading jelly on bread* with that uphill ski. Work on both sides. Then make big swooping S shapes as you go from turn to turn.

The Wedge Christie is just a temporary skill on the road to the parallel turn. Spend some time practicing nice wide slow-motion turns. Next, go a little faster and make the wedge smaller and smaller with each turn. Ease into French Fries earlier and earlier with those same turns.

YOUR ARMS!

match the tilt of your wings to the tilt of the slope

AIRPLANE WINGS

more weight on the DOWNHILL SKI

The actual transition between the Wedge Christie and a true parallel turn usually happens automatically when you start adding some speed to the process. Look out, 'cause the training wheels will come flying off!

RIGHT ON!

YEAH BABY, PERFECT BODY POSITION!

wings parallel to the slope

fine tuning yer AIRPLANE WINGS!

EWWW!

CLONK!

OOOPS! CRUMMY BODY POSITION!

wings tipped the wrong way

Mastering the Greens

Airplane turns

This is one of the best games to encourage skiers to properly pressure the downhill ski. You simply pretends to be an airplane. To do it right, the wings of the airplane should match (be parallel to) the slope you're on. To do this, your head and upper body will be bent over the downhill ski a little more than

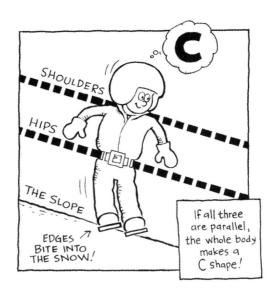

UPPER BODY and LOWER BODY can ROTATE SEPARATELY

the ZIPPER

LOOK where you wanna GO

POINT YER ZIPPER DOWNHILL

DOWN HILL

ALL THE TURNING HAPPENS DOWN LOW

TURN THE BOOTS and PANTS UNDER A STABLE UPPER BODY

the uphill ski. As the motions get smoother and less blocky, your whole body starts to look like a graceful C shape pointing downhill. This is the shape of an expert skier! The steeper the slope, the more the C shape helps you stay in control.

The zipper points downhill

Your jacket has a zipper that should be used like the laser guidance system for your whole system. Think of your pants and jacket as two distinct halves, and they each move differently. Your skis down at the snow will be moving back and forth with each turn, but your upper body should be stable and smooth. Focus on a *quiet upper body* by trying to keep your jacket zipper pointed downhill.

GETTING READY FOR THE BLUES

J turns

This describes the big curved J shape of the track you'll make with your skis in the snow. It's a fun way to introduce kids to the parallel stance, and it's another way they can stop.

Start out by skiing in a gliding Pizza straight down the slope, right in the fall line. Before you get going too fast, turn across the hill (out of the fall line) and make that curved part of the letter J. You'll come to a nice controlled stop with your skis pointing back uphill. It might help to have someone else make a big J turn first and then you can follow that track in the snow.

Can you do it in both directions? Can you see the big J in the snow? How far can you ski uphill? Can you make that bottom hook of the J really long? Can you go farther uphill in a Pizza or in French Fries position?

If you see your little one zooming too fast, you can holler "*turn uphill*" as a way to get them to do a nice controlled stop in J turn style.

Hockey stops

This is by far the coolest way to stop! Start out by making a bunch of J turns. Each time you do one make the bottom of the J shorter and shorter. The stopping will get quicker each time. Keep at it and you'll eventually stop so fast that you'll shoot a *rooster tail* of snow from your edges! The hockey

THE HOCKEY STOP

JUST LIKE THE "J" TURN

but...
you go from
FAST to STOP
without the
SLOW part!

a skill for
QUICK STOPPING

GO!

STOP!

POOF!

stop is just a J turn, only faster and more concentrated into a short little stopping zone.

The hockey stop makes a sharp crisp sound; you can throw snow downhill and dust your big brother! To really make the snow fly, you'll need to keep your balance forward and get low and aggressive.

This is a critical skill that needs to be mastered before heading up to Blue terrain where a wedge won't work for reliable stopping. Your edges are an important part of your skis, you'll need them to bite the snow. The hockey stop bites the snow hard!

Side slipping

This simple exercise will set you up with a whole slew of skills required for nice smooth French Fries (parallel) turns.

Start in the mountain stance with your skis across the fall line. Most of your weight will be on your downhill ski while your eyeballs and the jacket zipper are pointed down the hill. Slowly get TALL and gently roll your ankles a little downhill. Your edges will release and you'll start to slowly slip into the go line.

To stop slipping slowly, you'll need to get SMALL and tip your shins uphill to get your edges to grab the snow. With just a little practice, you'll be able to control your speed as you slip, but make sure you don't let your uphill ski get stuck in the snow! At first you'll have to concentrate on keeping it next to your other ski. Pretend that your ankles are tied together with a strong rubber band. Tip both shins uphill and keep that uphill pinkie toe in the snow. You can lightly brush that pinkie toe (and the ski) along the snow as they slip down the go line.

SIDE SLIPPING TIP!

You'll be subtly controlling your edges as they slide. Ease downhill as smoothly as possible and keep those skis in nice tidy French Fries.

The smooth slipping in this game is a great introduction to the skidding moves used in the beginner parallel turn. Not only that, but sometimes side slipping can get you out of trouble. Side slipping down a short steep section of a slope may be all that's needed to get smoothly past a zone of steep trickiness.

EASING
FORWARD
and
WEIGHTING
your
SKI TIPS

SIDE SLIPPING

EASING
BACK
and
WEIGHTING
your
SKI TAILS

THE
FALLING LEAF
MOTION

The falling leaf

This one starts just like the side slipping exercise, but instead of just sliding straight downhill, you should ease your balance forward toward your toes. You do this by lightly pressing your shins into the front of your boots. The goal is to slide both downhill *and* a little bit forward at the same time. Next, move your balance over your heels by leaning back a tiny bit. You'll start sliding the opposite direction. Get ready because you will actually be sliding downhill and *backward*. It's fun!

Find a rhythm—play with the pendulum sensation in your boots. When you get the swing of it, you can really feel the magic of how your toe to heel balance affects the skis. Style points for a nice stable upper body (or jacket zipper) facing downhill. Again, practice in both directions.

Checklist for skills
prepping for Blue runs

~ Find short steep sections to practice

~ Master getting up without help

~ Explore twisty-turny animal trails through the trees

~ Practice good habits

~ Show more angulation—the C shape

~ Work on J turns

~ Sharpen hockey stops

~ Try out side slipping

~ Slide through falling leaf

~ Perform garlands

~ Practice Wedge Christies

~ Keep French Fries parallel

~ Go in, get warm, drink hot chocolate

~ Have fun

Garlands

Sometimes these get called "chicken out" turns because you aren't fully turning in a new direction. You'll get the feeling of doing a real parallel turn in a nice controlled rhythm without having to deal with picking up speed in the fall line. This is a real confidence builder for easing into the parallel turn.

Find a spot where you can do a nice long French Fries traverse without worrying about traffic from above. Ski across a slope with your uphill edges *engaged* so they are biting the snow. Next, slowly get TALL, gently roll your ankles downhill, and *release* your edges. You'll feel yourself starting to tip down the slope. This is how a parallel turn starts. Just let it happen as you gently guide your feet downhill.

You'll pick up some speed but only for a second or two. Next, you'll *engage* those uphill edges again (pour out a little drink!) while turning your skis sideways to the hill. As soon as you do, you'll start to swoop out of the fall line and curve a little bit uphill. At first you might almost stop at the highest point.

You need to go back and forth between biting with your edges *at the bottom* of the swoop and smoothly gliding on the flat bottoms of their skis *at the top*. If you get into a good groove and add a tiny bit of speed, you should end each edging section with your skis pointed just a little bit uphill.

Drink in the smooth swoop of each motion. You should feel a magic weightless sensation at the highest point and a heavy pressure against your downhill ski at the lowest point.

Practice doing garlands both ways across the slope, think about how smooth you can make everything feel. When you check out your tracks, you should see a nice smooth arching line going up and down, up and down.

Garlands are the perfect lead-in to making you first parallel turns. Just embrace that exciting moment in the fall line and you'll will be there!

Side slipping, garlands, and hockey stops are essential skills to get a feel for turning the skis with French Fries only.

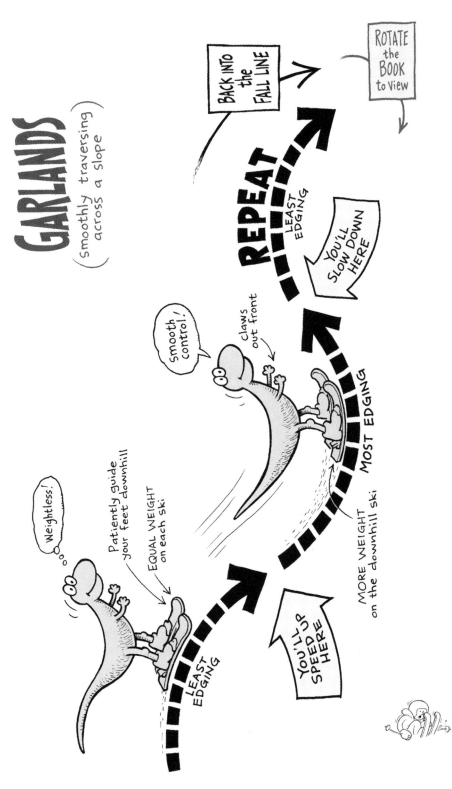

WHERE TO TOUCH THE SNOW
with yer poles

The parallel turn

It's a great big accomplishment when you can move beyond the Pizza wedge and start turning with French Fries. From here on out, you can use this advanced skill for pretty much all your skiing. If you have taken plenty of time to have fun with all the stuff up to this point, the parallel turn will come easily.

Start out with nice wide graceful giant S curves on easy terrain. Remember all the basics: keep your hands out front, look where you're going, get TALL at the beginning and SMALL at the end, balance over your outside ski, and use big toe-little toe to get the edges to bite the right amount. And smile!

The beginning parallel skier might make quick little movements that break up the graceful flow of the turn. The nice round shape of the S curve might look like a herky-jerky Z instead. It's still skiing, but it's not as smooth as it could be.

No need to do everything at once. Spread your moves out over the whole turn. Turn your feet and legs little by little, move between TALL and SMALL the whole time. Tip on and off your edges bit by bit. Find a flow and soon it'll feel smooth and graceful. When you feel good with the great big S turns try making snappy little s turns. You'll probably find

the
PARALLEL
TURN

HANDS
OUT
FRONT

ZIPPER
POINTING
DOWNHILL

NICE
"C"
SHAPE

UPHILL
EDGES
BITE
THE SNOW

NICE
SPRAY
OF SNOW!

NEXT
TURN

BIG
WIDE TURNS

SHORT LITTLE
TURNS

Checklist for the first Blue run

~ Lots of mileage under their belt on the hardest Greens

~ Solid mountain stance with no slipping

~ Solid hockey stops on both sides

~ Good to go side slipping and falling leaf

~ French Fries turn or narrow Wedge Christie

~ No problem getting up on their own

~ Knows the skier responsibility code

~ Always start out using the easiest way down

~ It's early in the day with plenty of energy in the tank

~ The child needs to be eager to head to the "Blues" (it's not just the parent's goal!)

that small to medium turns (*smedium*) will control your speed the best, especially on steeper Blue runs.

Now you have a whole cubby full of turns and tricks: Pizza turns, Wedge Christies, parallel turns, big turns, small turns, side slips, hockey stops, traverses, and more. Use 'em all! Keep that stable Pizza in your back pocket, because you never know when you might need to pull it out again. The Pizza might work better for moving through tight little animal trails.

THE DREADED POWER WEDGE!

LEG BURN

CHATTER

BLUE

IF IT'S TOO STEEP FOR PIZZA, YOU NEED FRENCH FRIES!

Avoiding the wedge in Blue terrain

Remember, over *Train* before over *Terrain'ing*. Skills that look pretty good on the Green slopes can quickly fall apart on a Blue run. Before heading out onto the steeper Blue runs, make sure to practice the skills listed above. Blue runs will probably start higher up on the mountain and will be longer than anything they've skied so far. Make sure they pace themselves and make sure to start out with plenty of energy in the tank.

Faced with a steep intimidating slope, kids that aren't ready will revert to huge Pizza wedges and lean way too far back. This *power wedge* won't work on steep slopes. These poor skiers will be fighting against the slope instead of skiing it. Little leg muscles burn out fast! This frightening experience can end a day of skiing and set progress back.

The easiest way down

If kids get in over their head on a slope that's too steep for comfortable skiing, you've made a mistake. This isn't fun. It can be downright scary. If you find you and your little skiers in this situation, your best option may be wall-to-wall traversing. Ski back and forth across the slope from one edge to the other. You may need to help them turn at the end of each traverse; this might mean picking 'em up and setting 'em down in the other direction. This is a slow and tiring process.

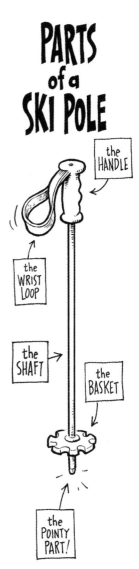

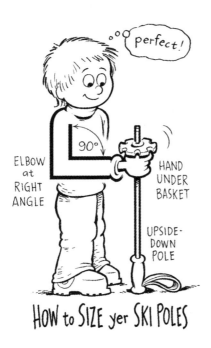

HOW to SIZE yer SKI POLES

Adding poles

If you've got a good handle on all the fundamental skills so far in this book, you can add poles into the mix. Poles can help you stay balanced in tricky terrain, lead you into your turns, and keep your rhythm and timing. Plus, they can enhance your shuffle on the flats and in the lift line.

the SKI TRACKS make a CURVY LINE

the POLE "TAP" marks are on the INSIDE of the TURN

UP THRU WRIST LOOP

1.

BACK DOWN

2.

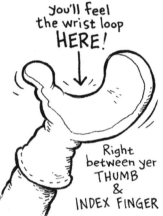

you'll feel the wrist loop **HERE!**

Right between yer THUMB & INDEX FINGER

HOW to USE yer WRIST LOOPS

The first step is just holding 'em while you're skiing, without even worrying about tapping the snow. Just like always, keep you hands up front on the steering wheel. No need to hold them up way up high, the poles can skitter on the snow as you ski.

The next step is to try what everyone calls the *pole plant*, though that's a crummy name because all you're really doing is just *touching* or *tapping*. It's a quick gentle motion. The tap should go *ping* and not *thud!*

This pole tapping should happen along with your turns. Try this for the first time on easy terrain. When you ease into the turn, it's the downhill hand that does the tapping.

Keep that hand on the steering wheel and just swing the basket forward using your wrists. Gently tap it down *toward* the turn on the *inside swoop* near your downhill skis. Ski past the tap mark, keeping your hands forward, and let the basket trail behind.

If you're on a bump run, just tap the bump and ski around it. It's like putting a candle on a cupcake.

Using ski poles might seem awkward at first. Make sure the poles are helping and not hindering your balance. If it's more fun skiing without poles, then just ski without 'em. Fun is more important than poles!

POLE "TAP" technique

HuH?

not too hard!

Cubs sleep on the outside of each turn!

KEEP MOVING!

You can tap baby polar bears on their head with each turn!

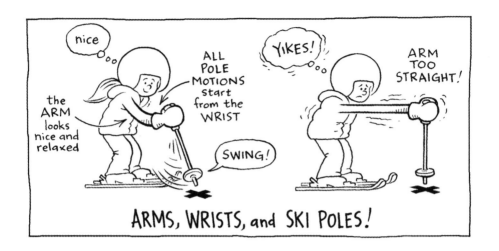

Mistakes with poles and tips to help

~ Supporting themselves as they ski (this is called *spidering*). If they are using their poles like crutches, then just ski some more without 'em and focus on balance.

~ Planting the uphill pole behind them as a way to stay in balance. Solve this by keeping their zipper pointed downhill.

~ Holding their hands too high. Letting 'em drag is totally okay!

~ Reaching with their arms—just swing from the wrist.

~ Tapping way off to the side. They should touch the snow a little in front of them near the downhill ski.

~ Ferociously stabbing the snow. Just a quick gentle tap is better. No grunting!

~ Tapping on the outside. Make sure they tap on the downhill or inside part of the turn. Sometimes beginners get confused and tap on the outside. It looks like they are paddling a canoe!

Next steps

From this point on, you're no longer a beginner. The next challenge will be mastering these skills and techniques. This book is only set up to introduce the fundamentals. Once these are in place, you can build on top of that foundation. Remember, expert skiers still keep their hands out front on the steering wheel and get TALL and get SMALL!

With these essentials in place, the rest of the mountain will start to open up for you. Explore! Try new terrain. Look for easy bumps. Find a fun race course. Sneak into some nicely spaced trees. Nibble away at new types of snow and different conditions. Try getting off the groomers and into untracked snow. Seek out the silky powder!

Find the limit of your comfort zone, and when the time is right, ease a little bit past that line.

Once you've mastered one skill, find a new challenge and master that one too! Y'wanna be super cool? Start telemark skiing! Skiing gets even more fun as you collect more and more new skills. So keep at it and have fun!

Index

About the Authors

Mike in 1967 with leather boots and bamboo poles

Mike Clelland!

Mike Clelland started skiing in 1967 in Northern Michigan. He has faint memories of that first day, but it obviously had a huge impact on the rest of his life. Mike continued skiing all throughout his youth and teen years. In 1981 he moved to New York City for college and then held a career as an illustrator with ad agencies along Madison Avenue. Although he loved city life, he'd always had the desire to move out West and live in the mountains for a winter as a ski bum. In the fall of 1986, Mike gave into that dream and ended up in Jackson Hole, Wyoming. That was 26 years ago, and (for the most part) he's been a ski bum ever since. He now lives in Victor, Idaho, in the shadow of the Tetons.

Free heels and a onesie

Alex Everett

Alex Everett is a PSIA level 3 alpine ski instructor and children's specialist at Jackson Hole Mountain Resort in Wyoming. He teaches all ages and backgrounds, from apprehensive "never-ever" three-year-olds to expert adults gunning for Corbet's Couloir. Alex grew up in the mountains of East Tennessee and learned to ski along the Appalachian Trail on the crest of the Tennessee-North Carolina border. The exciting, hardscrabble, billy-goat style of skiing on these rough trails planted the seed for future skiing adventures and a career as a NOLS instructor and mountain guide. Alex currently lives at the base of the Tetons in Victor, Idaho, and is very excited to get out skiing with his new little boy, Anderson.